Self-Surrender

TEN WAYS TO SUFFER WELL

IN UNION WITH GOD

Dewey J. Bjorkman

FOREWORD BY JAMES R. KURZYNSKI, STL

Self-Surrender
Ten Ways to Suffer Well in Union with God

Authored by Dewey J. Bjorkman
Foreword by Fr. James Kurzynski, STL
Edited by Ann Del Ponte
Prepared for Publication by Travis J. Vanden Heuvel

ISBN: 978-0-9969426-4-5

A Peregrino Press book

De Pere, Wisconsin

Peregrino Press seeks to publish material that is free of doctrinal or moral error. *Self-Surrender: Ten Ways to Suffer Well in Union with God* has been submitted to Church authorities in the Diocese of La Crosse, WI and has been granted the following:

Nihil obstat: Derik Sakowski, S.T.D.
                 Censor Deputatis

Imprimatur: +Most Rev. William Patrick Callahan
               Bishop of La Crosse, WI

               September 3, 2015

In Memory of
Robert "Bobby" Laxton

and

for
My Children

*May this book be a help to all those who want
to more closely attend to the hidden workings of the
Triune God in their own lives and in the lives of the people
with whom they live and to whom they minister.*

CONTENTS

Foreword   ix
Preface   xiii
Author's Note   xvii
Introduction   xix

Part One: Human Suffering and Divine Love

Suffering in the Depths of the Soul

I. Surrender: Striving for perfect self-surrender   3
II. Pray: Carry all of your burdens to the Source   17

The Imitation of Christ

III. Yield: To find your true end, walk Christ's life   29
IV. Imitate: Sharing in Christ's suffering humanity   43
V. Co-Suffer: Participation in God's compassion   61

Part Two: Suffering in Union with God

Suffering in the Moment of Grace

VI. Participate: God is One with us in our suffering   75
VII. Love: God's response to "Why, oh Lord?"   85

Union with God without Intermediary

VIII. Accept: Go out of yourself and into God   99
IX. Empathize: Resting in the One and the All   III
X. Unite: Meeting God without intermediary   125

Conclusion   141
Afterword   145
Endnotes   147
Bibliography   157

FOREWORD

FR. JAMES KURZYNSKI, STL

THERE ARE FEW THINGS in life more universal than the reality of human suffering. Whether one is a Catholic priest or Protestant minister, a theologian or teacher, an ordained deacon or a lay person who is committed to serving the sick, the homebound, and the dying, we all observe that suffering is indeed the ultimate equalizer. And every Christian in the pew must grapple with suffering, his or her own and that of others. This book addresses the subject of suffering by showing us that—far from being merely dark, foreboding, and destructive—suffering plays a central role in the Christian's saving conformation to life in God. The result is a refreshingly upbeat treatment of an intense topic. The joy of the Gospel shines through on every page.

As we all seek guidance in matters of faith, I have noticed that those who have a sincere desire to expand their mind beyond the basics of faith often meet a deflating end amid dense, technical language unique to theology, and writing styles so complicated that more than a theological dictionary is often needed just to finish the first few paragraphs. Rare in the academic world are texts that can create a bridge between the serious theologian and the serious novice who desires to plumb the depths of the mystical ocean we call theology. Dewey J. Bjorkman, one of my parishioners at Roncalli Newman Catholic Parish in La Crosse, Wisconsin, has successfully accomplished this delicate balancing act in this book, *Self-Surrender:*

Ten Ways to Suffer Well in Union with God. Dewey explores the theology of human suffering through the eyes of five Rhineland-Flemish pastors.

Each of the ten meditations begins with a clear overview of one particular aspect that is central to the Rhineland-Flemish theology of human suffering, followed by a faithful treatment of the primary texts that deal with that theme. What emerges is a book that has something for pastors, novices, and professional theologians. My confidence that this is so comes from my experience of having read through a late draft with our parish book club—an eclectic mix of blue collar workers, academic professionals, medical professionals, Catholics, non-Catholics, converts, and neighboring clergy. All of these personalities came to the same conclusion after reading Dewey's book: The text has enriched each of us and should be shared with a wider audience.

Sparked by a life-altering tragedy from his youth, Dewey introduces us to the pivotal voices that have accompanied him through his journey to understand the problem of human suffering. This journey initially led him to serve as a Lutheran pastor, but then he found himself being drawn to Catholicism, not as a movement of conversion in the popular sense but as a seamless transition, both intellectually and spiritually, through the ecumenical vision set forth by the Second Vatican Council. Dewey still treasures his Lutheran upbringing, seeing it, I think, as the necessary formation to embrace Catholicism not as "the other denomination" but as the completion of a journey that Luther himself desired as the endpoint of the Reformation: The reform and unification of the Church.

In this ecumenical spirit, Dewey and I found a kindred spirit in Lutheran theologian George Lindbeck. Lindbeck's book, *The Nature of Doctrine*, is a frequently discussed work. In it Lindbeck argues that ecumenical dialogue must go beyond focusing solely on attempts to arrive at agreement in doctrinal propositions. He says people also must do the hard work of delving into the density and beauty of our differences through a "cultural linguistic" framework. This approach of embracing the thickness of an intellectual tradition is a trademark of Bjorkman's text.

It was an honor to be asked to write the foreword to this book. Though this foreword is in my pen, it really is the voice of all of us who come together most Tuesdays in the fellowship hall of Roncalli Newman to explore current works of theology. In this spirit, I would recommend that this book be read as a private exploration on the meaning of human suffering, and I encourage you to create a community to journey through this text together, entering into a conversation about how we approach human suffering in the light of faith. My hope is that the five theologians of this work may walk with you through your life journey, just as they walk with Dewey, and now also accompany me in my ministry as a Catholic priest. Allow your mind to encounter the sacred through the Rhineland-Flemish Mystics. May that encounter give you insight into one of the most difficult questions of theology and life, the meaning and role of suffering in human existence.

Fr. James R. Kurzynski, STL
Author of *God's Canvas*

PREFACE

A CROSS AND A ROSE ARE ENGRAVED
INTO BOBBY'S HEADSTONE

MY PERSONAL WRESTLING WITH the question of God and human suffering began in earnest many years ago when as a teenager the sudden deaths of four of my friends in a car accident severely tested my courage and faith. I pretty much failed the test. As a young adult this loss, or rather my unfortunate response to it, stamped an indelible mark upon my inner life for years to come. Little did I know then that a group of medieval Christian theologians would prove to be so helpful to me in my spiritual journey that I would feel compelled (but joyfully so) to write this book about their achievement. The story begins almost five decades ago.

Early in the morning of May 6, 1967, I arose and readied myself to go to my part-time job at the cheese factory in Bangor, Wisconsin. I got there early, and seeing that Terry Nicoli had also arrived a bit early, I got into his car to chat with him while we awaited our start time. As seniors in high school he and I were only weeks away from graduation. Suddenly the music on the radio was interrupted by a news bulletin: "Four Bangor youth were killed last night in a car crash on County Trunk B just outside of La Crosse. Their names are being withheld, pending notification of next of kin." Terry and I looked at each other in disbelief. We soon learned the names of the dead: Randy, Peter, Ron, and Bobby. All of them were friends of mine; three were classmates. I was speechless. (In my youthful exuberance

I had thought us all immortal.) Bobby and I had been close friends for as long as I could remember; now he was gone. The passing of my friends sparked a spiritual crisis in my life. Although I was barely conscious of it at the time (tricking even myself), I resolved to soar above the pain, breathing pure spirit in foolish forgetfulness of the biblical reminder: "you are dust and to dust you shall return." (Gen 3:19b) This inner turmoil went largely unnoticed by others. I carried these unresolved issues with me into adulthood.

It was not until 1992 that I decided to travel to Wisconsin to visit the graves of my friends for the first time. I wanted to mark the anniversary of their passing. On March 23, 1992, I left my parents' house in Bangor and walked to St. Mary's Cemetery. It was a distance of a few short blocks; the journey had taken me a quarter of a century.

I said a little prayer at the graves of Randy, Ron, and Peter. As I stood before Bobby's grave, I noticed a life-sized crucifix which dominated the cemetery grounds; it had recently been painted silver to mark the 25th anniversary (or so it seemed to me). A cross and a rose had been engraved into Bobby's headstone. Unable to find words of my own, I said the Lord's Prayer. It is impossible to adequately convey what happened next. My spirit was enveloped in what I can only describe as the divine peace which surpasses all understanding. For a brief moment in time—but an *eternal* moment that through faith continues to live within me—recognition of God's gift of newness of life shone in my soul. My soaring spirit collapsed upon the earth—exhausted and at peace. Brightness returned.

***

In the aftermath of this moment of grace, I felt the need to integrate this experience into my religious beliefs, but this happened gradually, in God's good time. Over the years I looked for theological resources that could help me to—odd as it may sound—better understand the peace of God which surpasses all understanding. Second only to the Bible, it was the Rhineland-Flemish Mystics that helped me the most in this process. As I studied their books and sermons, a remarkable theology of suffering slowly came into view, prompting me to write this book.

AUTHOR'S NOTE

A SUGGESTION FOR HOW TO READ THIS BOOK

ON THE FIRST DAY OF classes at seminary, one of our professors posed this problem: "None of you have training in theology, yet you are going to be reading theology books written by authors who assume that you do have this training. What to do?" It was a rhetorical question. Without waiting for our response, he proceeded forthwith to offer his own. He suggested we try an approach to the reading of theology that he called the "percentage of newness" rule. I have found this rule to be so helpful in my own subsequent reading that I want to pass it on here.

My professor explained the rule this way: "When you begin to read a theology book you will soon discover the percentage of newness that the reading material contains for you." He divided books into two categories.

"Some books will be more or less a review of subjects that you already grasp, with little new content or terminology that presents a challenge. You know 80 or even 90% of what you are reading. You are in your comfort zone." He said the pleasure of reading these books is to "look for a few new interconnections between certain ideas that deepen your knowledge of this subject and help you to see them in a new light. There is gold in the 10% of the material that you do not know."

"In other books you will find that you have little knowledge of the subjects covered in them. You know 30, 20 or perhaps just 10% of the subject matter in these books. You are outside of your comfort zone." He said—and this is important—"Don't read these books expecting to understand all, or even most, of the material. That would be self-defeating. Read them with the aim to discover profound insights that, at least for now, must stand on their own. There is gold in those insights."

Finally, he suggested, "As you read, jot down significant insights, phrases, ideas, or sentences (along with the page number) in the front of the book. When finished, review the collected highlights and decide on the five most important insights that you noted. Circle the page number of each of these insights."

Our professor gave us good advice. I have followed his rule when reading many books over the years; it works. Today I can pick these books off the shelf and find references (which I noted on a Post-it) to words that speak to me anew, enriching my life once again.

Reader, I am confident that if you follow this rule while reading *Self-Surrender*, you will be blessed by the many nuggets of wisdom that speak of God's gracious communion with us in our suffering, even as we share in the sufferings of Christ.

INTRODUCTION

The Rhineland-Flemish theology of suffering acknowledges the secret, hidden reality of God's gracious work of love within the soul of every person that searches for God, and in finding God, lives in and with God and strives for perfect self-surrender in union with God.

THE REGION OF NORTHERN Europe that encompasses Germany, Switzerland, Alsace, Austria, and the lowlands brought forth in the 14th century theologians, philosophers, and mystics. Their mysticism was highly philosophical; their philosophy was at the service of faith. This book shows how Meister Eckhart (the Philosopher of Faith), Johannes Tauler (the Tender Pastor), Henry Suso (the Prophet of Wisdom), the Frankfurt Priest (the Admonishing Teacher), and John Ruusbroec (the Spiritual Director) fashioned a theology that sheds new light on the mystery of suffering.

Despite areas of divergence in their thinking, both in matters of emphasis and in substance, the family resemblance of their thought reveals a characteristic Rhineland-Flemish spirituality. In ten meditations (I–X), two for each of the five mystics, I present and comment on their pastoral theology, exploring the wise counsel they bring to the subject of suffering. Readers, you are invited to become full participants by adding your interpretations of these texts to my own. This is not an exhaustive treatment of this topic, but each meditation develops one particular aspect of this theology of suffering that I think is deserving of special attention. The result is the discovery of *Ten Ways to Suffer Well in Union with* God.

Presenting the Rhineland-Flemish theology of suffering and translating it into language that brings its message home to people today involved three aspects.

First, I gather together into one accessible volume certain key texts in which these theologians express their theology of suffering. Retrieving these texts from relative obscurity, I make the resources of this spiritual tradition more readily available for ministry today. This assemblage of texts provides many practical helps for daily ministry that both edify and console. As a result, this book can serve as a kind of Preparation Manual to help people build their house upon the rock, so that when the winds of suffering beat upon the house, the house will stand.

Second, I organize these primary source materials according to their main themes and present commentary and theological reflections upon the text. References from secondary sources are included, bringing other Christian theologians into the conversation in order to clarify a line of reasoning, prompt further reflections, or enrich the discussion.

Third, I recover a significant contribution that these theologians make to the Church regarding the role of suffering in Christian life. They insist that, for the Christian, suffering involves two inseparable aspects: the usual active sense of suffering that involves endurance of hardship and pain, and a passive sense that involves striving in faith for perfect self-surrender in spiritual detachment from the things of the world. This nuanced understanding of suffering is not a theological innovation, but the consistent and disciplined way that these theologians apply this two-sided definition of suffering to the life of faith *is* new. In these meditations I show how this understanding of suffering (which involves both active and passive aspects) is integrated into a thoroughly Christianized Neoplatonic theology. I also show how this interpretation of the meaning of suffering renders sublime interpretations of a number of Scripture verses[1] that beautifully weave the experience of suffering into the fabric of Christian discipleship.

I have had a long history of association with the thought of these theologians. My first contact with the theology of the Rhineland

Mystics came in 1986 when a former seminary classmate gave me books by Meister Eckhart and Johannes Tauler. Because of my personal interests as a theologian, I read their sermons with a special eye to see how they addressed the problem of suffering. I was drawn to the work of Tauler, but at this stage I found Eckhart's theology of the mystical ground to be impenetrable. My encounter with him would have to wait.

What struck me most about Tauler's theology was how radically his theological anthropology penetrates to the mystery of what it means to be human. Tauler taught that human beings must carry their burdens to the Source, to the ground. It is in the ground of the soul where a person can find "God in God and light in light." That is where blossom and fruit are one. (See Meditation II)

For Tauler, the three stages of the spiritual life are jubilation, desolation, and divinization. He instructs those souls who are undergoing spiritual desolation to embrace all of the suffering that comes to them, whether it is deserved or undeserved. "Welcome bitter affliction, full of grace!" (VIII)

In May of 1992, I read a little book written by an anonymous 14th century German priest who served the Teutonic Order of Knights and lived in Frankfurt. Tradition has given it the title *Theologia Deutsch* or *Theologia Germanica*. The teachings in this book captivated me. One key text reads, "And all this the soul does in silence, resting in its ground, and in a secret, hidden, suffering empathy, enabling it to carry all, to suffer with all." (IX) The elusive phrase "resting in its ground" clearly points to some sort of union with God, a union that happens in silence and that occurs in the hidden recesses of the soul that is open to God. And this union involves an odd kind of suffering, a "suffering empathy."

The context of this passage indicates that the call for a believer to imitate Christ is related in some ineffable way to this so-called "ground." The Frankfurt Priest is adamant that those who would like to know the true goal of life must "walk the right path toward it, namely Christ's life." (III) Once again, a Rhineland theologian impressed me by the way he addressed the subject of suffering.

Two years later I was delighted to discover John Ruusbroec's *Spiritual Espousals* while reading Evelyn Underhill's book, *Mysticism*. Ruusbroec's treatment of the virtues includes an insight into how human participation in the divine compassion carries with it an unavoidable wounding of the human heart. He writes, "Compassion is a wounding of the heart which love extends to all without distinction. This wound cannot be healed as long as anyone still suffers." Indeed. (V) Ruusbroec's treatise concludes with a description of the summit of mystical life: union with God without intermediaries. But for Ruusbroec this union does not leave suffering behind. Instead, sacrificial suffering (dying to self) stands at the very heart of a person's participation in the *mysterion*. (X) His theology strives to unite the bridal mysticism of love (of St. Bernard and Hadewijch of Antwerp) with his own Trinitarian mysticism of essence that was influenced by Eckhart. Ruusbroec's profound idea of death and rebirth by means of divine love encouraged me to continue to investigate the Rhineland-Flemish Mystics.

In 2006 I found a fresh translation of Henry Suso's *Wisdom's Watch Upon the Hours* (*Horologium Sapientiae*). This Latin work contains much of the material from his earlier book, *Life of the Servant*, which he had written in his vernacular German. In this book Suso gave me new insight into the question of theodicy. He argued that when the soul awakens to its true vocation, the stubborn human demand for a theodicy—a justification of God in the face of suffering—is redirected by grace into the sphere of the unfathomable love of God. (VII) His *Little Book of Eternal Wisdom* also helped me to understand the role the imitation of Christ must play in Christian discipleship. He taught that in order for a person to reach the heights of divinity, he must first pass through "the gate of Christ's suffering humanity." (IV)

Finally, in 2009 Bernard McGinn edited *The Complete Mystical Works of Meister Eckhart*. I warmed to the thought of Eckhart, who exerted so much influence on the other four Rhineland-Flemish theologians. Eckhart's sermons helped me to understand his notion of the ground of the soul, which contains within it a cluster of elements (there is more here than meets the eye) that is fundamental to his theological anthropology.

In one such sermon he sets forth this thesis: God has established that suffering is a necessary attendant to the attainment of happiness. (I) The McGinn volume includes Eckhart's *Book of Divine Comfort*. In it Eckhart shows how suffering relates to the transcendent Oneness of God. He argues that God is One, so whatever a good man suffers for God's sake, he suffers in God; so God is with him when he is suffering. He concludes, "What more could a sufferer want?" (VI)

These remarks foreshadow some of the principal themes of this series of meditations. I can only begin to hint at the spiritual power that is everywhere apparent in the actual texts, in which our five pastors speak to us directly—in the immediacy of their own words. Care must be taken to receive their message. I suggest limiting one's reading to one meditation per sitting to slow down the process and allow time for prayer and reflection. Such attentiveness allows one to note how the various insights of these mystics interrelate in a way that suggests the outlines of a coherent theology of suffering. With that in mind, but without getting too far ahead of ourselves, we begin by asking a preliminary question: What is the secret of their shared theological vision?

We recall the thanksgiving prayer of Jesus, "At that time Jesus declared, 'I thank you, Father, Lord of heaven and earth, that you have hidden these things from the wise and understanding and revealed them to infants; yes, Father, for such was your gracious will.'" (Mat 11:25) Christians have long puzzled over this prayer. Is Jesus saying the good news of the Kingdom of God is meant only for a few people? The five theologians who are our chief guides in this venture help us to understand this mysterious prayer. To their minds, the Gospel reveals *a hidden mystery of love*. It is this *mysterion* that constitutes the substance of their vision of the Gospel.

What is the nature of this *mysterion*? Servais Pinckaers provides this working definition:

> The Greek word *mysterion* means something hidden, secret. It is the property of love to enter into the secret depths of the

beloved, to establish a certain communication between persons on the plane of the mysterious and unfathomable. The preoccupation of Christian mysticism has always been love, its growth, and the different stages leading to its perfection, as well as its most concrete manifestations. Unfortunately, mysticism has been excluded from Christian ethics, as if it were intended only for the elite and as if morality could forego this dimension without cutting itself off from the very strength and dynamism of charity.[2]

The reality that is hidden in the revelation—the reality for which Jesus gives thanks to the Father in His prayer—is the advent of the Kingdom of God. The in-breaking of the Kingdom is discernible only by God-given faith. This message of love creates division when it enters into the world. God's love is resisted and denied. The so-called "wise" and "understanding" people of this world miss the point of their very existence (e.g. I Cor 1:18-31).

In light of God's revelation, it becomes clear that it is only those who admit their absolute dependency upon God in trusting surrender who are caught up into the sphere of God's gracious reign. This surrender is the basis for much that the Rhineland Mystics have to teach about suffering. Meister Eckhart and the other four mystics were able to discover meaning and significance in suffering by drawing upon the wisdom they discerned in "the plan of the mystery (*mysterion*) hidden for ages in God, who created all things." (Eph 3:9b)

The meditative mood of this commentary reflects the tenor of Rhineland-Flemish spirituality. The tone is that of prayerful contemplation, similar to that of Thomas Merton's book *Seeds*. This approach respects a basic presupposition of these pastors: Before God it is required that a person assumes an inner attitude of detachment, quiet, and receptivity; then, God's Word comes by stealth.

The Rhineland-Flemish theology of suffering acknowledges the secret, hidden reality of God's gracious work of love within the soul of every person who searches for God, and in finding God, lives in and with God and strives for perfect self-surrender in union with God.

This book has been written out of the conviction that readers who sit at the feet of these theologians will learn much about the mystery of suffering and more still about the even deeper mystery of the love of God. It is this revelatory interaction between the twin mysteries of human suffering and divine love that propel this study forward, gradually bringing into focus the shape of the Rhineland-Flemish theology of human suffering.

There is a mystical dimension to orthodox Christianity that is attested to in the Bible but is nonetheless often ignored or denied. Christians must drink from the Source; mysticism speaks to this need. And most significantly, there is a mystical dimension to the Triune God's response to human suffering. The wondrous depth of God's compassionate communion with suffering humanity in the incarnation of Jesus Christ is central to the Gospel. The Rhineland-Flemish theology of suffering is a rich resource that can deepen and revitalize the Church's reception of the good news of Jesus Christ.

***

Many people supported me in this undertaking. I am grateful to Thomas F. O'Meara, O. P. for providing indispensable editorial guidance as he responded to three separate drafts of this book. Stan Grotegut first called my attention to the work of Tauler and Eckhart. Dean Stroud closely read two drafts of the manuscript, offering many valuable suggestions.

Greg Wegner helped to simplify the format and to strengthen the meditations that deal with the Frankfurt Priest. Derik Sakowski offered several acute observations. Kevin Thornton gave me advice on the ins and outs of preparing a good book proposal. Donna Ables, Jeanell Carlson-Bjorkman, Linnea Bjorkman, Timothy Bjorkman, Micah Juliot, and Fr. Mark Pierce read early manuscripts and provided helpful suggestions and encouragement.

Special thanks go to Travis J. Vanden Heuvel at Peregrino Press for publishing my book and for his belief in this project. And I heartily thank my editor, Ann Del Ponte, for helping to shape the manuscript into a book.

Alongside of my work as a lay theologian, I have had the good fortune over the years to work with scores of fellow booksellers in the course of my career in bookselling. I thank them for providing me with a supportive environment within which to do research, reflect, and write. Joel McKinzey (formerly of McKinzey-White Booksellers of Colorado Springs) and my current co-workers at Barnes and Noble Booksellers in La Crosse, Wisconsin, were especially helpful.

I want to take this opportunity to express my gratitude to three of my teachers from my early years of Christian formation as a Lutheran. Rev. Reginald A. Siegler taught me daily Confirmation classes at St. Paul's Ev. Lutheran School, in Bangor, Wisconsin, that centered on the Bible and the memorization of Luther's *Small Catechism*. Duane A. Priebe allowed me to take three independent study classes with him at Wartburg Theological Seminary in Dubuque, Iowa, an unforgettable experience that was a highlight of my four years of work on a M.Div. degree. Carl E. Braaten served as my advisor while I worked on a Th.M. degree at the Lutheran School of Theology at Chicago. His *Lectures on Christology*, which dealt with many of the principal themes of Christology, made a deep impression on me and inspired me to do my best to become his kind of pastoral theologian.

Today, I write this series of meditations as a Roman Catholic lay person, having been received into that Communion at the Easter Vigil in 2007. The Roman Catholic theologians that I draw upon for spiritual sustenance in this book confirm my profound indebtedness to them. Chief among them are our five Rhineland-Flemish theologians. I want to thank Fr. James Kurzynski, my former pastor at Roncalli Newman Parish, for writing the foreword and for inviting me to present a late draft of my manuscript to our parish book group. In the course of seven sessions, we delved into the thought of each mystic. The discussions were wide ranging, and the group gave valuable feedback that significantly strengthened the book. My sincere thanks go to Fr. Kurzynski, Dick Berendes, Mary Garves, Jane Intress (of blessed memory), Teresa Meara, Rose Peterson, M. Therese Regner, Amy Schleeter, Dean Stroud, Greg Wegner, and Paula Wegner, all of whom contributed to the discussions.

Finally, I am thankful to God for my parents, Milly and DuWayne ("Dewey") Bjorkman, my sister, Carolyn Herman, and for the love of family and friends. This volume is dedicated to my beloved children and to the memory of my childhood friend, Robert "Bobby" Laxton.

***

It is fitting that the writing of this book should be completed on this Feast Day, for it was on the road to Damascus that Christ confirmed the doctrine of the Mystical Body of Christ (which contains within it a beautiful theology of suffering) when He asked Paul: "Saul, Saul, why do you persecute me?" This day also has great ecumenical significance in that it was on this day in 1959, on the final day of the Week of Prayer for Christian Unity, that Pope John XXIII went to the Basilica of St. Paul Outside the Walls to announce Vatican II.

The Conversion of Saint Paul, Apostle
January 25, 2017

PART ONE

Human Suffering
and Divine Love

MEDITATION I

THE WAY OF SURRENDER

Our bliss lies not in our activity but in being passive to God. For just as God is more excellent than creatures, by so much is God's work more excellent than ours. It was from His immeasurable love that God set our happiness in suffering because suffering plays an essential role in the saving process of our conversion to life in God. This conversion occurs by faith—human participation in the eternal birth of the Word in the ground of the soul.

MY WORK ON THIS manuscript coincided with the three-year period when my nephew battled Lou Gehrig's disease, ALS. Scott passed away in 2013 on the day after Thanksgiving. To see a strong man of 38 years slowly succumb to this disease was a vivid reminder that we human beings are all vulnerable to suffering. Scott was courageous to the end, more than once declaring to me, "God's grace is enough." In his living and in his dying he witnessed to how important it is that we give heed to these words of Jesus: "Everyone then who hears these words of mine and does them will be like a wise man who built his house upon the rock; and the rain fell, and the floods came, and the winds blew and beat upon that house, but it did not fall, because it had been founded upon the rock." (Mat. 7:24-25)

In this meditation, Meister Eckhart teaches us, similarly to Scott's witness, that when we suffer greatly it is important that we not over-think about our suffering. We dare not brood about suffering. Faith entails a childlike trust in God. In the light of faith we can learn to see our suffering as a difficult but necessary part of our conversion to life in God. This is due to the role that suffering plays in our vocation to surrender our lives completely into the hands of God. This perfect self-surrender—which is itself a kind of suffering—is the path to true happiness. Eckhart insists that by God's grace we need not be overwhelmed by our suffering or miss the chance that God is giving to us to find some great blessing precisely in and through our suffering.

So let us begin our encounter with Meister Eckhart.[3] The next few pages lay the foundation for much that is to follow because our other four Rhineland-Flemish theologians were in varying degrees influenced by Eckhart. In these pages I introduce his vital concept of the ground of the soul largely in his own words simply because I cannot improve upon the clarity of his presentation. A word of caution: While Eckhart is a consummate teacher, his arguments are often dense and packed with intricate insights that are at times difficult to understand. But be of good cheer! The rest of the book is, for the most part, less demanding.

My advice to the reader is to continue to read on, but to periodically revisit this section until a clear understanding of his central teaching is gained. Such perseverance will pay its dividends, as it did for me.

Eckhart focuses on the subject of God and human suffering in several sermons as well as in his *Book of Divine Comfort*. In this initial meditation we look at three sermons that provide an introduction to the ideas that shape his theology of suffering.[4] In a key sermon Eckhart develops his thesis of the eternal birth of the Word in the human soul.

First, Eckhart speaks of the place where this eternal Word is spoken:

[It] is in the purest thing that the soul is capable of, in the noblest part, the ground—indeed, in the very essence of the soul which is the soul's most secret part. There is the silent 'middle,' for no creature ever entered there and no image, nor has the soul there either activity or understanding; therefore she is not aware there of any image, whether of herself or of any other creature. (30)

[This part of the soul] is by nature receptive to nothing save only the divine essence, without mediation. Here God enters the soul with His all, not merely with a part. God enters here the ground of the soul. None can touch the ground of the soul but God alone…In consequence, there is nothing so unknown to the soul as herself. (31)

If it be asked how the Father gives birth to the Son in the soul, Eckhart's answer is "*by my faith*, but just as He gives birth to him in eternity—no more, no less." (32) [emphasis added] This statement is central to understanding Eckhart; we will return to it repeatedly.

Second, Eckhart asks what a person must contribute in order for this birth to occur:

[He says that his teaching holds good for those] who have so absorbed and assimilated the essence of all virtues that these virtues emanate from them naturally, without their seeking; and above all there must dwell in them the worthy life and lofty teachings of our Lord Jesus Christ. They must know that the very best and noblest attainment in this life is to be silent and let God work and speak within. When the powers have been completely withdrawn from all their works and images, then the Word is spoken. (33)

Third, he speaks of the Word that makes God known in the depths of the soul:

About this, the wise man said, "In the middle of the night when all things were quiet silence, there was spoken to me a hidden word. It came like a thief by stealth." (Wisdom 18:14-15). Why does he call it a word, when it was hidden? The nature of a word is to reveal what is hidden. It revealed itself to me and shone forth before me, declaring something to me and making God known to me, and therefore it is called a Word. Yet what it *was,* remained hidden from me. That was its stealthy coming in a whispering stillness to reveal itself. See, just because it is hidden one must and should always pursue it. It shone forth, and yet was hidden; we are meant to yearn and sigh for it. (34-35)

Fourth, Eckhart speaks of the fruit of this birth of the Word in the soul:

> The Son of the heavenly Father is not born alone in this darkness, which is His own: you too can be born of the same heavenly Father and of none other, and to you too He will give power. Now observe how great the use is! For all the truth learned by all the masters by their own intellect and understanding, or ever to be learned till Doomsday, they never had the slightest inkling of this knowledge and this ground. Though it may be called nescience, an unknowing, yet there is in it more than in all knowing and understanding without it, for this unknowing lures and attracts you from all understood things, and from yourself as well. This is what Christ meant when He said, "Whoever will not deny himself and will not leave his father and mother, and is not estranged from all these, is not worthy of me." (Matt 10:37), as though He were to say, he who does not abandon creaturely externals can be neither conceived nor born in this divine birth. But divesting yourself of yourself and of everything external does truly give it to you. (36)

***

In another important sermon, Eckhart preaches on the text from Matt. 2:2: "Where is he who is born king of the Jews?" He remarks,

"Now I say, as I have often said before, that this eternal birth occurs in the soul precisely as it does in eternity, no more and no less, for it is *one* birth, and this birth occurs in the essence and ground of the soul." (39) He goes on to insist that in order for this Word to make itself heard, a person "must come to a forgetting and an unknowing. There must be a stillness and a silence...We cannot serve this Word better than in stillness and in silence: *there* we can hear it, and there too we will understand it aright—in the unknowing. To him who knows nothing it appears and reveals itself." (43) But one might object to this on the belief that God would not want us to find our salvation in ignorance. Eckhart explains:

> Where there is ignorance there is a lack, something is missing, a man is brutish, an ape, a fool, and remains so long as he is ignorant. Ah, but here we must come to a *transformed* knowledge, and this unknowing must not come from ignorance, but rather from *knowing* we must get to this unknowing. And through holding ourselves passive in this we are more perfect than if we were active. (43)

Then, having laid a sufficient foundation, Eckhart is ready to deliver one of his most important teachings as he addresses the question of human suffering, but with a twist:

> But our bliss lies not in our activity, but in being passive to God. For just as God is more excellent than creatures, by so much is God's work more excellent than mine. It was from His immeasurable love that God set our happiness in suffering [*leiden*], for we undergo more than we act, and receive incomparably more than we give; and each gift that we receive prepares us to receive yet another gift, indeed a greater one, and every divine gift further increases our receptivity and the desire to receive something yet higher and greater. Therefore some teachers say that it is in *this* respect the soul is commensurate with God. For just as God is boundless in giving, so too

the soul is boundless in receiving and conceiving. And just as God is omnipotent to act, so too the soul is no less profound to suffer; and thus she is transformed with God and in God. God *must* act and the soul must suffer, He must know and love Himself in her; she must know with His knowledge and love with His love, and thus she is far more with what is His than with her own, and so too her bliss is more dependent on His action than on her own. (44)

How shall we interpret this decisive text? The first thing we notice is that for Eckhart suffering does not have the same primary meaning it has in modern culture. Suffering does not refer first and foremost to the physical pain and psychic anguish of the subject. Instead, in a deeper spiritual sense, Eckhart says, *suffering is a person's trusting surrender, in a posture of inner passivity that waits expectantly for God to do His saving work in the soul.* It follows from this that suffering is not simply negative; in fact, it can be supremely positive. Indeed, due to sin and the disordered state of the world, it is God's will that suffering play a central role in Christian discipleship, mirroring the cross of Christ. Out of this suffering comes newness of life: salvation.

To help us understand this peculiar sort of suffering, it is helpful to consult Josef Schmidt, who remarks how Eckhart and Tauler use the verb *leiden* (to suffer):

> Detachment [*gelassenheit*] entails, for instance, the notion of active passivity, a condition poignantly mirrored in the verb *leiden* where various meanings (to suffer, to like, to pass through, etc.) are matched by the functional duality of expressing something both transitively and intransitively and becoming an almost matching expression of '**striving for perfect self-surrender.**' [bold emphasis added] [5]

This concise formulation (striving for perfect self-surrender) sharpens our understanding of the Rhineland-Flemish theology of suffering and provides the guiding theme of this study. With this expression Josef Schmidt allows that Eckhart and Tauler do often use the term "suffer" (*leiden*) to refer to hardship, bodily pain, or mental anguish. This common reference to suffering has two components: the subject and the object that is required to complete the sense. "I suffered a miscarriage." "My friend suffers from pneumonia." "Those who have shingles suffer great pain." "She suffered the loss of her leg." "Through much suffering he came to see the error of his ways." But crucially, Josef Schmidt discerns a *functional duality* in the way the verb "to suffer" is used by Eckhart and Tauler. He argues that when they refer to suffering there is a dual meaning that includes both *actio* (action), a subject's endurance of hardship and pain, and *passio* (passivity), a stilling action that is limited to the subject, with no direct object. The point is that there is a spiritual state of mind wherein the believer strives for perfect self-surrender, strives to be free of all created things and creatures, seeking only detachment (*gelassenheit*), with no object. The believer abandons things of this world in active passivity, suffering only to receive, not act. In his essay *On Detachment*, Eckhart develops this aspect of suffering. He writes:

> Now I ask, 'What is the object of pure detachment?' My answer is that the object of pure detachment is neither *this* nor *that*. It rests on absolutely nothing, and I will tell you why: pure detachment rests on the highest, and he is at his highest in whom God can work all His will. But God cannot work all His will in all hearts, for although God is almighty, He can only work where He finds readiness or creates it...He works as He finds readiness and receptivity. Now in whatever heart there is *this* or *that*, there may be something in 'this' or 'that' which God cannot bring to the highest peak. And so, if the heart is to be ready to receive the highest, it must rest on absolutely nothing, and in that lies the greatest potentiality which can exist. For when the detached heart rests on the highest, that can only be on nothing, since that has the greatest receptivity. (571-572)

For Eckhart, the Christian must suffer, that is, humbly surrender to the will of God and cease all self-striving, allowing God to do His gracious work in the soul. In modern culture the idea of receptive passivity is frowned upon; it is said that people must act, initiate, create, subdue, and assert. But for Eckhart, when we have to do with God, "God must act and the soul must suffer..." (44) Human creatures do not relate to God as they do to one another or to other creatures, no! God, as Creator and Redeemer, acts; God's creatures receive in active passivity.

Picking up again from Eckhart's sermon on suffering as active passivity, he goes on to say:

> In this way your unknowing is not a lack but your chief perfection, and your suffering your highest activity. And so in this way you must cast aside all your deeds and silence your faculties, if you really wish to experience this birth in you. If you would find the newborn king, you must outstrip and abandon all else that you might find.
>
> That we may outstrip and cast behind us all things unpleasing to the newborn king, may He help us who became a human child in order that we might become the children of God. (44)

Suffering must not be viewed one-sidedly as something dire that is merely to be avoided. In the deepest sense suffering is humankind's "highest activity" because it is basic to human dignity to submit to God and allow God to be all in all. This submission entails complete surrender to God. *Striving for perfect self-surrender* provides the overarching theme that guides these meditations. Our presentation of the *Ten Ways to Suffer Well in Union with God*—Surrender, Pray, Yield, Imitate, Co-suffer, Participate, Love, Accept, Empathize, and Unite—will gradually flesh out the meaning of this theme, illuminating suffering in new and edifying ways.

***

In a sermon on I John 3:1, Meister Eckhart speaks of the believer's "sonship" in the Father:

> Man has a twofold birth: one *into* the world, and one *out* of the world, which is spiritual and into God. Do you want to know if your child is born, and if he is naked—whether you have in fact become God's son? If you grieve in your heart for anything, even on account of sin, your child is not yet born. If your heart is sore you are not yet a mother—but you *are* in labor and your time is near. So do not despair if you grieve for yourself or your friend—though it is not yet born, it is near to birth. But the child is fully born when a man's heart grieves for nothing: *then* a man has the essence and the nature and the substance and the wisdom and the joy and all that God has. *Then* the very being of the Son of God is ours and in us and we attain to the very essence of God. (75)

Eckhart describes how it is that a sinful human being can become a child of God. For him this process has no analogy on the human plane. He answers by quoting John 1:12-13: "But to all who received him he gave power to become children of God; who were born, not of blood nor of the will of the flesh nor of the will of man, but *of God*." The soul detaches itself from outward things and empties itself in active passivity and is born of God. God comes into the ground of the soul, and the Son is born therein. This rebirth transforms suffering because of the life-giving Spirit of the Son in her soul. The person of faith will no longer grieve in her heart for anything because her pain has been taken up into God.[6]

Here I will pause for a moment and shift the discussion a bit. One of the tasks before us in these meditations is to retrieve the main aspects of the Rhineland-Flemish theology of suffering and to bring these ideas into fruitful contact with theology in our day. Our initial venture will connect Eckhart's discussion above (about conversion to life in God) with Hans Urs von Balthasar's masterful description of the same event. This example illustrates the continuing relevance of Eckhart's thought and will bring Eckhart's position into sharper focus. I will quote Balthasar in three sections, stopping only for brief comments.

> When the individual believer is drawn into the whole Church, he is baptized 'into the death' of Christ (Rom 6:3), in order to be led down into a depth and definitiveness of self-surrender that remains unattainable for him as a limited human being but which he makes his aim in the act of faith and which he longs to see carried out, because he wishes to 'appropriate' to himself the total self-giving of God, opening up the whole space for it and giving it the adequate response which it intends. As a believer he does not remain passive: in his baptism, he is admitted into the sphere of the Spirit of God and of the Church, and he declares himself in agreement with this Spirit and makes him his own.[7]

Notice Hans Urs von Balthasar's language of active passivity: baptized into; drawn into; led down; longs to see carried out; appropriating the total self-giving of God; admitted into. Yet, the initiate is led to self-surrender and declares agreement with the Spirit. He continues:

> He lets himself be 'led' and 'driven' by the Spirit, but not as by a foreign spirit (a 'spirit of slavery'): this is his own Spirit, the 'Spirit of sonship,' who makes us cry out: "Abba, beloved Father!" (Rom 8:15). And when Paul continues: "This Spirit confirms to our spirit that we are children of God" (8:16), then this confirmation lies beyond monologue and dialogue: the fact that *we* ourselves cry 'Father!' confirms to us that we are crying out of the Spirit of God and consequently are his children: the dialogue is not between our spirit and the *Pneuma*, but between our spirit, borne by the *Pneuma*, and the Father, a dialogue in which the *Pneuma* cannot be other than the

Pneuma of the Son, in whom we have come to share in sonship: 'because we now are sons, God sent the Spirit of his Son into our hearts, who cries out: "Abba, beloved Father!"'[8]

A believer lets herself be led and driven by the Spirit, but this is the Spirit of adoption—and so this is her *own* Spirit that makes her cry, "Abba, Father!" Since she cries out "Father!" in the power of the Spirit, she shows herself to be a child of God. In a delicate insight Hans Urs von Balthasar describes how the believer's spirit is borne by the *Pnuema* of Christ into communion with the Father and thereby consummates the process of her adoption as a child of God.

Balthasar further describes the conversion of the sinner to a life that is centered in God by sounding two of the fundamental themes of Neoplatonic Christian theology: the eternal generation of the Son (John 1:13) and the return of the sinner to her Origin—to life in God—that was already predestined for her "before the foundation of the world." (Eph. 1:4f) We have seen how Meister Eckhart has interpreted the event of the eternal birth of the word in the ground of a believer's soul as participation in the eternal generation of the Son. (Meditation II will show how Johannes Tauler builds upon Eckhart's idea of the salvific return of the sinner to her Origin, to life in God.)

Balthasar concludes his account of conversion with this statement:

> But it is precisely this that demonstrates the *Pneuma* to be the Spirit of the Father, because it is only through him that we can be sons (with the Son), drawn into the event of the eternal generation of the Son (Jn 1:13). But thereby we arrive precisely at the place that was already predestined for us beforehand 'before the foundation of the world' (Eph 1:4f), so little alienated from ourselves that it is by entering into the absolute love that we first find ourselves.[9]

This necessarily brief discussion has exhibited the striking similarities between the conversion theologies of Hans Urs von Balthasar and Meister Eckhart. The initiate is given new life in the Son and empowered by the Spirit to cry out: Abba! Having been adopted by God, the child of God finds that her sufferings are taken up into the life of God. This is the God-given gift of faith—human participation in the eternal birth of the Word in the ground of the soul—that re-vivifies the human spirit, bringing new life.

***

Our initial meditation highlights one of Meister Eckhart's central teachings: human happiness is inextricably connected to suffering. Eckhart says, "It was from His immeasurable love that God has set our happiness in suffering." (44) It is happiness that knows the true goal: union with God. And this union *can* come to fruition in this life. This union altogether transforms suffering. The following words from Eckhart summarize this opening meditation and set the stage for the next one:

> When you have completely stripped yourself of your own self, and all things and every kind of attachment, and have transferred, made over, and abandoned yourself to God in utter faith and perfect love, then whatever is born in you or touches you, within or without, joyful or sorrowful, sour or sweet, that is no longer yours, it is altogether your God's to whom you have abandoned yourself…God bears the Word in the soul, and the soul conceives it and passes it on to her powers in varied guise: now as desire, now as good intent, now as charity, now as gratitude, or however it may affect you. It is all His, and not yours at all. (51)

The inseparable relation between suffering (*leiden*) and faith is now laid bare. For Eckhart suffering is in essence a striving for perfect self-surrender to God. And this abandonment to God "in utter faith and perfect love" on the part of believers is possible because God has already demonstrated His trustworthiness to them in and through the faithfulness of Jesus Christ. While faith includes a free intellectual assent (*assensus*) to a body of divine revelation that takes the form of knowledge (*notitia*), trust (*fiducia*) takes center stage. For only trust in God that is given life by God's steadfast love and faithfulness can empower people to strive for perfect self-surrender. This is the reason Eckhart can say that the Father gives birth to the Son in the soul and that He does this "*by my faith*, but just as He gives birth to him in eternity—no more, no less." (32) [emphasis added] Faith is the light of God illuminating the innermost ground of the soul, bringing new life. In the moment that a person suffers this repentance and the human spirit turns to God in the ground of the soul, grace is born. From that moment forward any suffering that a child of God undergoes is undergone in Christ and with Christ. Then, says Eckhart, the suffering "is all His, and not yours at all." (51)

MEDITATION II

THE WAY OF PRAYER

Do not waste time over created things, which in themselves are nothing, but bring yourself and all your concerns back to the Source. There it is that true praise of God is born, and it bears fruit in the ground of your soul. There, blossom and fruit are one, and you will find God in God, and light in light. Carry all your burdens of soul or body back to the Source, which is God. Offer them to Him and yourself with them.

THE THEOLOGY OF JOHANNES Tauler is centered on prayer. His teachings are a treasure trove of practical theology for daily ministry. The summary statement above points to God's way with us, to how God saves, and to that reality which is most real of all: love. This meditation, like the first and the sixth, is heavily philosophical; but the aim is life-giving love.

In His Sermon on the Mount, Jesus said, "The eye is the lamp of the body. So, if your eye is sound, your whole body will be full of light; but if your eye is not sound, your whole body will be full of darkness. If then the light in you is darkness, how great is the darkness!" (Mat. 6:22) If we are cut off from God, we are cut off from life. In God's light we live. But before we embark upon this meditation, we must first guard against a common misunderstanding about this "light."

Gerhard Ebeling points out that the Greeks had two different ways of approaching this light: *nous* and *pneuma*. The term *nous* (mind) refers to, as Ebeling would have it, "the unchanging clarity of the light in which things stand for the gaze of the observer"—to timeless truth.[10] Often this so-called "perfect light" puffs a person up with false pride (e.g. Col 2:18). (Jerome A. Miller can even say, "[There are] two demonic rivals for a mind in crisis—the despair of nihilism and the Light of Perfect Knowledge."[11]) When Tauler says that sufferers can find "God in God, and light in light" he is not speaking of *nous*, but of *pneuma* (spirit). In the New Testament *pneuma* suggests the uncontrollable blowing of the wind, which mysteriously catches one up in its movement. (e.g. Jn 3:8; Acts 2) *Pneuma* is a living power that grants to the human spirit the capacity, the courage, to bless and to affirm temporal existence despite the many trials and hardships of life. The *holy Pneuma* is a renewing Spirit that brings life-giving light and turns the heart of stone into a heart of flesh. (Ps 51:10; Ez 36:26)

***

Johannes Tauler[12] once preached a sermon in which he spoke of the indwelling of God in the ground of the soul and how the Son brings new life to the human spirit:

> Other masters [i.e. Eckhart] say…that the perfection lies in the utterly inward, hidden and deepest ground of the soul, the ground in which the soul has God substantively (*wesentlich*), actively (*wurklich*), and essentially (*isteklich*), and where God works and is and enjoys Himself. One could so little separate himself from this ground as he could separate himself. For it is by God's ordination (*ewige ordenunge*) that He has established (*geordent hat*) that He neither can nor desires to separate Himself from this ground. Thus, in the ground [of the soul] this ground has all by grace that God has by nature. And should man permit, and turn himself to the ground, grace would be born. Apart from this turning, all other ways, even the highest,

can accomplish nothing.[13]

***

In another sermon Tauler describes this event of faith in the depths of the soul:

> Anyone who wants to experience this must turn inward, away from the activities of his faculties, both exterior and interior, away from all imaginations and all the notions he has acquired from outside himself, and sink and lose himself in the depths. Then the power of the Father will come and call the soul into Himself through His only-begotten Son, and as the Son is born of the Father and returns to the Father, so a man is born of the Father in the Son, becoming one with Him... Our Lord was speaking of this when He said: "This day have I begotten you, through and in My Son."[14]

Commenting upon Ephesians 4:23: "...and be renewed in the spirit of your mind," Johannes Tauler says,

> Children, that [rightly turned and directed mind] is the ground wherein the true image of the holy trinity is inwardly and secretly laid, and it is so noble that one can give it no proper name. Sometimes one calls it a foundation, sometimes a tower of the soul. For just as inadequately as one can give a proper name to God, so inadequate is the effort to name the ground. Should one see how God dwells in the ground, he would be truly blessed by what he beholds. The intimacy and filial relationship which God has there is so inexpressibly great that one can neither speak nor have spoken of it except from boldness.[15]

Tauler also speaks of the exalted role that the human mind plays in the spiritual life. The intellect is recognized to be a power that when rightly ordered can connect us to God:

> Now St. Paul says, 'you should be renewed in the spirit of your *gemuete* [mind].' When this *gemuete* is ordered, it has an inclination back to this ground, wherein, far above the powers of the soul, the image is present. And this returning operation of the *gemuete* is as noble and exalted above the powers of the soul as a full vat of wine is over one drop. In this *gemuete* one should renew himself by constantly drawing himself back into the ground, and turning with an active love and disposition directly to God without any mediation. The *gemuete* certainly has the power to do this. It can well have a constant adherence to and an uninterrupted disposition toward the ground which is not within the capabilities of the powers of the soul. This renewal should be in the spirit of the *gemuete*. Since God is a Spirit, the created spirit should unite itself, then direct itself to and sink itself into the uncreated Spirit of God with a permissive *gemuete*. Thus, as man was eternally God in God in his uncreatedness, so should he draw himself completely, with his createdness, back again.[16]

Implicit in this line of thinking is the presupposition that God and humanity enjoy a common spirituality that is rooted in the precreaturely, uncreated origins of the human soul in God. (Eph 1:4) Humanity, created in the image of God, longs to return to this Origin. Tauler explains:

> The spirit of man has many names in accordance with its operation and the perspectives from which it is considered. Sometimes the spirit means soul; this is the case to the extent to which the spirit pours life into the body, and is thus in every member of the body, giving it movement and life. Sometimes the soul is called spirit, and then it has so intimate a filial relationship (*sipschaft*) with God that it is immeasurably great. For God is a spirit and the soul is a spirit; whence the soul

has an eternal inclination and orientation back to its original ground. As a result of this common spirituality...[only like can know and love like] the soul inclines and turns itself back again to the origin, to the likeness. This inclination is never extinguished, not even in those who are damned.[17]

Only like can know and love like. While faith cannot possess, control, or manipulate this indwelling of the *imago trinitatis* in the ground of the soul, this presence is a condition of the possibility of any human knowledge of God or love for God. "For with you is the fountain of life; in your light we see light." (Ps 36:9) Also the Apostle Paul, "...no one comprehends the thoughts of God except the Spirit of God." (I Cor 2:11b) Hans Urs von Balthasar makes the same point: "Faith is the light of God becoming luminous in man, for, in his triune intimacy, God is known only by God."[18] The Spirit of God and the human spirit have an intimate filial relationship because the human soul originates in God. Tauler is agreeing with Meister Eckhart on this central question. James A. Wiseman, OSB summarizes Eckhart on this matter:

> [Eckhart taught that] there is a twofold aspect of each of us: our virtual being (*esse virtual*), preexistent in the mind of God from all eternity and so sharing in the divine power (*virtus*), and our formal being (*esse formale*), originating only at the time of our creation as beings in space and time.[19]

In light of this discussion, it is helpful to examine three of Tauler's sermons. In these sermons he shows how God's gracious indwelling in the ground of the soul is able to transform human suffering, whether it is suffering of body, mind, or spirit.

First, there is the following statement from his sermon on the Ascension:

> Do not waste time over created things, which in themselves are nothing, but bring yourself and all your concerns back to

the Source. There it is that true praise of God is born, and it bears fruit in the depths [i.e. ground] of your soul. There, blossom and fruit are one, and you will find God in God, and light in light. Carry all your burdens of soul or body, whatever they may be or whatever their origin, back to this Source, which is God. Offer them to Him and yourself with them.[20]

God comforts His people when burdens are taken in prayer to the Source in the ground of the soul, for that is where the indwelling of God gives strength to those who suffer.

Second, in another sermon he teaches the following:

It is when we have great and heavy sorrows to bear that we can tell whether we have [the] true light or not. At such times, those who truly love God take refuge in Him, bear it all patiently and accept it as coming from Him. Either they endure their sorrow with Him and in Him, or else they lose all their sorrow in Him; for if we enter deep into God's heart, we find that sorrow there is not sorrow, but is turned to joy and bliss... [On the other hand with] God's false lovers, it is quite otherwise. When they are afflicted with sorrow they do not know which way to turn. They run up and down looking for help and advice and comfort, and when they do not find it they are plunged into despair and doubt.[21]

For those who flee to God in time of need, suffering is undergone in union with God. In the mystery of faith, this can make it possible for the sufferer's sorrow to turn to joy.

Third, Tauler contends that God often uses suffering to lift us up to higher things:

[At times the bitter myrrh of suffering] is sent by God. It may be any kind of suffering, inward or outward. If only we would accept this myrrh lovingly and with all our hearts, just as God gives it to us, what a life of joy would begin for us, what happiness and peace it would bring… Sometimes people say to me, "Father, I am in great trouble and distress"; and when I tell them that they should be thankful they say, "Oh no—because I am afraid I have brought it on myself through my own wickedness."

My dear, dear child, set your heart at rest. Whether you have deserved it or not, take your suffering as coming from God, thank Him for it and be at peace and at rest. Every myrrh sent by God has been specially arranged to lift us up through suffering to higher things… If only we will accept as we ought these myrrhs which are God's gift to us, He will shape us to His own design with many a stroke of the brush, many a tint of suffering, until He has finished us to His perfect satisfaction.[22]

Pastor Tauler teaches his flock, "If only we would accept this myrrh [of suffering] lovingly and with all our hearts…what happiness and peace it would bring." This acceptance, this striving for perfect self-surrender, is another way, the way of prayer, to suffer well in union with God.

When God graciously dwells in the ground of the soul, the Giver becomes the Gift of redemption. Conversely, where this presence is lacking, there is a subtle pang of aimlessness. As Henri de Lubac has so incisively remarked: "In me, a real and personal human being, in my concrete nature…the 'desire to see God' cannot be permanently frustrated without an essential suffering…"[23] In the ground of the soul, the human spirit hungers for the holy and yearns to see God in a final state which tradition has named *beatitude*. Human beings long to truly understand the *telos* (or goal) of human life and what it is that constitutes human fulfillment. Human beings must neither smother the inborn desire to "see God" (Mat 5:8) or worse, explain it away as the denial of death or a naïve wish for pie in the sky by and by.

Influenced by Tauler and others, Romano Guardini discerns the vital connection between the indwelling of God in the human soul and one's capacity to deal with suffering:

For somewhere in every individual is that which the spiritual masters called the ground of the soul, the spirit's edge, the inner spark. It is not difficult to imagine that the silent divine eloquence continues unbrokenly in all of us, un-narrowed by the limits of form or sound; that this isolated existence of ours in the midst of so much strangeness, this dangling in senseless chance is only bearable because constantly, whether we register them or not, secret tidings of reassurance trickle through to us. We have been taught that we owe our existence to the eternal word of the Father; thus we may well suppose that on the ground-floor of our being the quiet converse between ourselves and him continues, and that it is from here that we draw our certainty of life's sense.

…Perhaps we understand things only because we hear in them the secret stream of the hidden, eternal word. I really believe that this is so, otherwise, we should be unable to comprehend and to love; we should be excluded from the great unity. If this intrinsic reassurance of God were to be suddenly plucked from all things, destroying them, how terrifying all the incomprehensible, unlovable instruments of death and sorrow about us would be![24]

The indwelling of the image of the Trinity and the hidden eternal word in the ground of the soul constitute the foundation upon which the tender human spirit can resist succumbing to faint-heartedness and despair. Sad to say, human beings too often do not attend to this word, but instead attempt to overcome estrangement from God by other means. This will be to no avail. What is needed is an obedient listening to the eternal word of the Father that speaks to the soul in its very ground. This word is the Word—the Logos of God—Jesus. (John 1:1)

Guardini is not alone in his appreciation of Tauler. Tauler's mysticism is Christ-mysticism that emphasizes that the essence of faith entails the *constant reliance* of the believer upon the risen Christ. Like

Guardini, Martin Luther was influenced by Tauler. In his 1515 lectures on the Book of Romans, Luther reflects a Taulerian understanding of faith in his commentary on Romans 5:1-2, "Therefore, since we are justified by faith, we have peace with God through our Lord Jesus Christ. Through him we have access to this grace in which we stand..." For purposes of analysis, Luther's commentary is divided here into two segments. In the first segment that which Luther had in common with Tauler comes to the fore. Luther says:

> In the first place, the statement is directed against those who are so presumptuous as to believe that they can approach God without Christ, as if it were sufficient for them to have believed, as if thus by faith alone, but not through Christ, but beside Christ, as if beyond Christ they no longer needed Him after accepting the grace of justification...It is necessary to emphasize both points: "through faith" and "through Christ," so that we do and suffer everything which we possibly can in faith in Christ. And yet in all of these activities we must confess that we are unprofitable servants, believing that only through Christ are we made worthy to approach God. For in all the works of faith we must strive to make ourselves worthy of Christ and His righteousness as our protection and refuge. "Therefore, since we are justified by faith" and our sins are forgiven, "we have access and peace," but only "through our Lord Jesus Christ."[25]

Here Luther emphasizes the believer's constant reliance upon Jesus Christ who alone provides access to God and the peace of God. In this he is in agreement with Tauler. Yet in segment two, Luther explicitly eliminates the goal of ascending to God as a legitimate one. On the contrary, he denies that mysticism can offer access to God. He parts ways with Tauler and with *transformational* mysticism as a whole when he says:

> This also applies to those who follow the mystical theology

and struggle in inner darkness, omitting all pictures of Christ's suffering, wishing to hear and contemplate only the uncreated Word Himself, but not having first been justified and purged in the eyes of their heart through the incarnate Word. For the incarnate Word is first necessary for the purity of the heart, and only when one has this purity, can he through this Word be taken up spiritually into the uncreated Word. But who is there who thinks that he dares aspire to this level unless he is called and led into the rapture by God, as was the case with the apostle Paul, or unless he is "taken up with Peter, James, and John, his brother" (Matt.17:1)? In brief, this rapture is not called an "access."[26]

It is clear that already in 1515 Martin Luther was rejecting the idea of a saving direct union with God without intermediary in favor of a *penitential* mysticism that affirms the abiding presence of Christ who lives in the heart of every contrite believer. It would seem that Heiko A. Oberman is correct when he says, "[Luther] read Tauler and the *Theologia Germanica* as striking examples of genuine, personal, living theology, not as exponents of mysticism."[27] Nevertheless, one can hear in Luther's 1515 lectures on Romans the echo of Tauler's insistence on the necessity of a constant reliance of the believer upon Christ as the only mediator between God and man.

In sharp contrast to Luther's 1515 position on mysticism (one that he hardens in later years), Eckhart, Suso, and Tauler follow their fellow Dominican Albert the Great and his student, Thomas Aquinas. Thomas picks up on certain aspects of Pauline theology; for instance, when the Apostle Paul speaks of the way of transformation in I Cor 3:18. "And all of us, with unveiled faces, seeing the glory of the Lord as though reflected in a mirror, are being transformed into the same image from one degree of glory to another; for this comes from the Lord, the Spirit."

To closely paraphrase Servais Pinckaers' helpful summary of Thomas' anthropology, Christ is the perfect image of God (Col 1:15). A human being's image is imperfect, but still bears a resemblance to God because of his capacity for attaining God by the distinctive activities of knowledge and love. In human beings the image of God is dynamic, not static. Thomas outlines what he sees as the three stages in the process of the human resemblance of God. In the first stage human beings possess a rational nature and an aptitude for knowing and loving God. This is indestructible. In the second stage there may be a progressive conformation to God through grace that has its source in the substance of the soul and unfolds through the workings of the theological virtues of faith, hope, and love. The third stage is the coming into the perfect knowledge and love of God that is reserved for the final state of blessedness in heaven which will be the perfect image, the resemblance in glory.[28] Transformational mysticism is central for Thomas and for our five Rhineland-Flemish theologians.

That Johannes Tauler's Christ-mysticism entails a constant reliance upon the risen Christ is vividly confirmed in a third sermon by Tauler that is based on John 12:32: "If I be lifted up, I will draw all things [Tauler's loose translation] to myself." The work of Christ that brings new life to believers is tied to the cross of Christ:

> Here [John] refers to man who bears a likeness to all created things. There are many who find the Cross by means of much suffering and numerous trials, and this is the way God draws them to Himself.[29]

For Tauler, the merciful God can use suffering as an occasion for redemption. But if sufferers refuse to face up to their affliction, the opportunity to experience God's mercy is lost to them. The courage of faith empowers believers to raise their suffering up to God in prayer:

> But this suffering must not be merely encountered; it must be lifted up, exalted, as it is on today's feast. If we looked into our hearts we would find the Cross there twenty times a day in many painful incidents and afflictions by which we are indeed crucified if only we understood the sign. Instead we try

to avoid taking up the Cross, and that way we commit a grave injustice.[30]

Finally, Tauler shows believers how suffering can become redemptive:

> One should assume that burden freely, lift it right up to God, and then accept it as one's very own, be the circumstance external or internal, corporal or spiritual. Thus one is drawn into God, into Him who will draw all things to Himself, as He said He would now that He is lifted up.[31]

When sufferers are "drawn into God," they share in the sufferings of Christ. They also share in all of the blessings of life in God. The Crucified One draws suffering human beings into the Life of the Trinity. As children of the Father, through the Son, in the power of the Spirit, the sufferings of believers are taken up into Trinitarian bliss and joy.

MEDITATION III

THE WAY OF YIELDING

The true end of human life can only be obtained by faith, be-cause, as yet, no one knows how to say anything about what the true end is. Yet, those who would like to know must walk the right path toward it, namely, Christ's life. The Christian trusts that it is enough to know that the imitation of Christ and His cross-shaped life does lead to the goal.

THE READER WHO HAS persevered through the lively intensity of the first two meditations may well be asking, "So what's the big deal? I accept the fact that life includes suffering." My response to this question is twofold. First, do we really accept the *magnitude* of the presence of suffering in our world? And second, it is spiritually dangerous for us to set aside the subject of suffering because of the central role that suffering plays in our conversion to life in God. A recognition of this connection between suffering and our eternal salvation unites us with God as we undergo suffering, often imbuing it with great meaning that grants to us unexpected joy.

In this third meditation we learn from the Frankfurt Priest that it is basic to human nature for a person to desire to grow and develop toward...toward what? He answers: toward God. The human spirit, despite the fall into sin, is called upon to cooperate with the divine Spirit in God's work of salvation. This cooperation is essential if we are to realize the possibility of a beautiful unfolding of our lives that actually progresses forward in time toward the goal of beatitude, toward full communion with God.

Spiritual life is not stagnant, for if it were, it would mean that the power of the Gospel remains extrinsic to humanity's most fundamental need: to grow into communion with God. But this would be monstrous; God is closer to us than we are to ourselves. God does not leave us bereft of His loving presence deep within our souls: "If a man loves me he will keep my word, and my Father will love him, and we will come to him and make our home with him." (Jn 14: 23) We are not alone in our suffering. In this meditation the Frankfurt Priest shows us how to persevere in our confrontation with suffering and how God will lighten our spirit with divine love. He shows us the path to follow: the life of Christ.

> [If] we are to yield to God in such stillness we must at the same time be subject to everything, including not only God but also ourselves and all created beings, nothing barred…
>
> …In and during it all the soul takes no recourse to evasion, excuse, resistance, or vengefulness. The newborn soul rather speaks through it all in loving, humble, true compassion: "Father, forgive them; for they know not what they do"….for the paths mentioned above were followed perfectly and wholly in the life of Christ until the end of His bodily life on earth. There is consequently no better path or preparation to the dear life of Jesus Christ than that selfsame life and its practice to the extent possible…All that has been said here…is a description of a road, or road signs, to the true end. But no one knows how to say anything about what the true end is. Yet, he who would like to know may he walk the right path toward it, namely Christ's life. (88-89)[32]

The Frankfurt Priest[33] teaches that those who want to know the true goal of human life should walk the right path toward it: Christ's life. Jesus extended a similar call, "If any want to become my

followers, let them deny themselves and take up their cross and follow me." (Mark 8:34) This is Christ's bid to recall fallen humankind
out of its estrangement from God. In this third meditation the focus
is on what it means for people to imitate Christ by living out of the
power of His life. The Frankfurt Priest gives his answer to the question: What is the shape of a life that conforms to Christ's life? His
answer to this question identifies one of the central aspects of the
Rhineland-Flemish theology of human suffering, namely, the imitation of Christ in His cross-shaped life.

I begin with the Frankfurt Priest's programmatic statement regarding the nature of human sin that gave rise to the need for God's
plan of salvation in Christ.

First, the Frankfurt Priest speaks of sin as "the I, the Me and the
Mine":

> We are used to saying that Adam was lost and fell because
> he ate that apple. I say it was because of his presumption and
> because of his I and his Mine, his Me and the like. He could
> have eaten seven apples, yet had this not been connected with
> his presumption, he would not have fallen. But he fell at the
> moment his presumption occurred and that could have hap-
> pened even if he had not bitten into a single apple. But listen—
> I have fallen a hundred times deeper than Adam and strayed a
> hundred times further. No humans in the world could make
> amends for or undo Adam's fall and apostasy. (62)

Second, he outlines God's plan of salvation to rescue humankind
from sin:

> How, then, shall the fall be redeemed? It must be amended
> like Adam's fall and by the same one who amended Adam's fall,
> and in the same manner. By whom or in what manner did this
> healing take place? Man could not do it without God and God
> has not designed to do it without man. Hence God assumed
> human nature or humanity. He became humanized and man

became divinized. That is the way the amends were made.

My fall must be amended in the same way. I cannot do it without God and God does not command or will it without me. For if it is to happen, God must become humanized in me. This means that God takes unto Himself everything that is in me, from within and without, so that there is nothing in me that resists God or obstructs His work…In this return and healing I can, may, or shall do nothing from myself but simply let it happen. This means that God alone works and I suffer His work and His will to take place.

When I do not suffer this to occur but let my I and my Me rule, I hinder God from working alone without obstruction. (62-63)

For the Frankfurt Priest salvation means nothing less than becoming divinized, to become one with God. He says that in order for this to happen, "God must become humanized in me. This means that God takes unto Himself everything that is in me, from within and without, so that there is nothing in me that resists God or obstructs His work…"

The believer's role is to simply let God do His saving work within the soul. To be sure, human beings can block this saving work through the stubborn self-assertion of the ego, so the only remedy is to *yield* to the will of God. This yielding is a form of suffering—of striving for perfect self-surrender—that is another way for a believer to suffer well in union with God.

This raises the question as to how human beings can be freed from this egocentricity. From whence comes the power for a fallen human being to yield to God's will? How does God break through sin? Before we hear the Frankfurt Priest's answer to this question, consider these preliminary remarks that set the stage for a consideration of his teachings.

In the Athanasian Creed the Church confesses that Jesus is "perfect God" and "perfect man." "Perfect man" signifies, in part, that the Son assumed human nature and lived His earthly life in humble obedience to His God and Father. He lived as the incarnate Son of the Creator. Because He was true man (an authentic human being), His life was an exemplary one that others can take as the model for their lives. Looking upon Him they behold their Exemplar who is at the same time the Son of God, the Righteous One, who gave Himself up for the life of the world. Thus, the sense in which Jesus is an exemplar needs to be clearly distinguished from the way believers may wish to emulate other human beings because Jesus alone is sinless; everyone else is flawed and in need of redemption. It is in this spirit that Dietrich von Hildebrand speaks of a right understanding of the imitation of Christ:

> Sometimes, one can hear or read, "act in every situation in the same way as Christ would have acted." But this is a wrong formulation of the imitation of Christ…The imitation of Christ should rather be expressed in the words "Act in a way which can stand the test in a confrontation with Christ,"… or in the words "act always in the spirit of Christ."[34]

The Frankfurt Priest makes it clear that it is through Christ that humanity is divinized. Let us look to the four Gospels for some clues as to how this mystery of salvation unfolds. In the Gospel accounts, the Church, in the power of the Spirit, discerns the revelation of God in Jesus of Nazareth viewed from the vantage point of the post-Easter community. Those who come into the life-giving sphere of His lordship find their true selves there. Vatican II says, "[It] is only in the mystery of the Word incarnate that light is shed on the mystery of humankind. For Adam, the first human being, was a representation of the future, [Rom 5:14b] namely, of Christ the Lord. It is Christ, the last Adam, who fully discloses humankind to itself and unfolds its noble calling by revealing the mystery of the Father and the Father's love."[35] Although He is the Eternal Son, Jesus of Nazareth begins His public ministry humbly with the message of the good news of the imminent in-breaking of the Kingdom of God. He is careful to differentiate Himself from the Father, even rejecting the title "good Master"

(Mk 10:18), saying that God alone is good. In John 5:19 Jesus says, "The Son can do nothing of his own accord, but only what he sees the Father doing." The main characteristic of Jesus' ministry is His obedience to the Father. From the time of His temptation in the wilderness right up through His prayer at the Garden of Gethsemane, He prays, "not my will, but Thy will be done."

Wolfhart Pannenberg draws the appropriate Christological conclusions from the way that Jesus conducts His ministry when he says:

> The self-distinction of Jesus from the Father…can be described as his self-emptying and self-humbling… We have here two essential features of Jesus as the new man, the man of obedience to God as distinct from the sin of Adam, who wanted to be like God and who thus forfeited the fellowship with God for which he was destined.[36]

When Jesus undergoes three temptations (Luke 4:1-13) in the wilderness, He models how an exemplary human life can actually limit the scope of human suffering. He resists the temptation to place His need for safety and security above His spiritual needs and looks for support in the Word of the Father. "One does not live by bread alone." (v.4) He resists becoming enraptured by the power and glory of this world by refusing to set Himself up as His own god. "Worship the Lord your God, and serve only him." (v.8) He resists putting the power of God to the test and instead places His life trustingly into God's hands. "Do not put the Lord your God to the test." (v.12) Jesus models the will of the Father who requires that humanity resist the temptation to place security above obedience, vain-glory and power-seeking above worship, and fear and anxiety above trust in God. Jesus thereby manifests His humble station as the New Adam who is obedient to the will of God.

The Frankfurt Priest notices this remarkable insistence by Jesus that the focus of His ministry be entirely upon the will of the Father and not upon His own will. And He draws the appropriate conclusions as to how this relates to Christian discipleship:

So we certainly know at what point God takes over in man. *Wherever Christ and His true followers are, we are sure to find deep humility and poverty of spirit and a chastised and reflective mind. In this mood there is bound to be a secret, hidden sorrow and suffering lasting into bodily death...* [emphasis added]

Nature and self recoil from the life-in-God and hold to the life of false lawless freedom, as I also said. Now, aided by such natural reluctance an Adam or a devil appears on the scene, armed with a subterfuge: "You are almost saying that Christ became void of His own self and everything connected with it. Yet He often spoke of His self and glorified His self in one way or another."

Answer: Where Truth is active in deed and in will, her will and desire and work revolve around just one thing: that she may become known and manifest. This was the truth in Christ; both word and work were parts of it. But the best and most profitable of it all is this: He was free from these word and work events, just as free as He was from other things around Him, in the sense that He never claimed them as His own. But you say: "So there was after all a 'wherefore,' an ulterior motive, in Christ?" I answer: You ask the sun, "Why do you shine?" She says, "I have to shine and can do nothing else. It is my nature. It is in me to shine. But I am at the same time free from this nature and from the shining for I do not emit my own light." This is the way it is with God and Christ and all that is godly and belongs to God. It wills, works, desires, nothing but the Good, for the sake of the Good. There is no other "wherefore." (95-96)

Christ in His "word and work" sought in freedom only to manifest the light of God. But, says the Frankfurt Priest, many who hear the Gospel seek to cast doubt on Christ's motives. This is so because "[the sinful human] nature and self recoil from the life-in-God and hold to the life of false lawless freedom." It wants no part of "secret, hidden sorrow." But the truth is that there can be no such evasion of suffering. On the contrary, he speaks of the *increase* of suffering that will inevitably come upon Christians as they develop a heightened awareness of the sin and disobedience that permeates our fallen world:

> If someone were genuinely and wholly obedient (as we believe that Christ was, else he would not be Christ), all human disobedience around him would be a source of inner, bitter suffering to such a person. All disobedience is nothing but resistance to God…
>
> The person who experiences in his own suffering and feeling that disobedience is a source of sorrowing for God and that it is against God would rather suffer a hundred deaths, vicariously, in order for disobedience to die, even if it were in just one single soul, and for obedience to be born again. I grant you, then, that no one lives totally and purely in this obedience, the way Christ did. It is, however, possible for man to approach and come so close to it that he can be called—and can in fact be—godly and divinized.
>
> *And the closer man approaches divine obedience and the more godly and divinized he becomes, the more he will feel the pain over disobedience, sin, and unrighteousness, and the more such waywardness will hurt him and the more keenly he will suffer.* [emphasis added] (80)

Reflecting on this closely argued statement we notice that the Frankfurt Priest begins by stating the unremarkable fact that all forms of disobedience to God cause the true disciple of Christ a great deal of sorrow and pain, but concludes with a statement that startles and surprises: "[The] closer man approaches divine obedience and the more godly and divinized he becomes…the more such waywardness will hurt him and the more keenly he will suffer." His thesis is that growth toward divinization brings more pain, not less. And that it is only the work of God's Spirit within a believer's soul that can open his heart, first to recognize and then to undergo ever deepening forms of suffering. In the following comments he develops this thesis in greater detail, suggesting that a Christian theology of suffering must defend three assertions. First, believers must share in the hidden anguish that Christ experiences due to human disobedience. Second, this anguish will persist for as long as a Christian lives. And third, this sorrow is God's work and only secondarily the work of believers. Here is the relevant text:

> Let us say again: Into God as God no pain, grief, or dislike can come. Yet God is grieved on account of man's sin. Since grief cannot be in God outside the creature, it occurs when God is in man or in a divinized man. Sin is such a pain to God, it saddens Him so much, that He would Himself be tortured and bodily die so that He might thereby wipe out a person's sin. If we asked God if He would rather live so that sin should remain, or die in order to destroy sin, He would choose death. For God feels more pain over man's sin and it gives Him more grief than His own torture and death.
>
> Now, if one person's sin causes God pain, how much more, then, the sins of all men? So you see how deeply man grieves God with his sins. Where God is man or in a divinized person one does not grieve over anything but sin. Nothing else gives real pain. For all that is or occurs without sin, that is what God will have and be.
>
> *Yet grief and sorrow over sin should and must remain in a divinized person until he leaves his body in death, even if he were to live until the latter day, or forever. From this came Christ's hidden anguish of which no one reports or knows but Christ Himself. Therefore we call it what it is: hidden.* [emphasis added]
>
> This hidden sorrow over man's sinful condition is an attribute of God's that He has chosen and that He is pleased to see in man. But it is God's attribute above all. *Sorrow over sin does not finally belong to man; man is not himself capable of it.* [emphasis added] Wherever God can bring it about in

us, it is the most pleasing and most appropriate but at the same time the most bitter and heavy undertaking on which we can enter.

What we have been describing here is one of God's attributes, which he yet would like to see in man. For it is in man that it should be practiced and put into effect. The true Light teaches us about sorrow over sin; it teaches us, moreover, that man, in whom it is put into effect and practiced, should claim that divine mood for himself as little as though he were not there. (109-110)

By affirming this inevitable hidden anguish, the Frankfurt Priest exposes those false followers of Christ who mislead others when they claim that they already enjoy a share in the resurrection life of Christ without the cross, without suffering. They are deceived:

It is true that God can be known by no one or nothing but God. When natural man fancies that he knows God, he is thereby saying he is God. In fact, he presents himself as God and wants to be so considered. He thinks he richly deserves all good things that come his way and he believes he has a right to everything. He is convinced that he has risen above all the things of the world, that he has conquered and so forth. He even looks on himself as having transcended Christ and the Christ life.

But he actually denigrates the Christ life in his imagined detachment. For in reality he has no desire to be Christ; he wants to be the eternal God. How come? Because Christ and His life are contrary and burdensome to all nature and natural man wants no part of it. Natural man desires to be God in eternity, not man. Or he may wish to be the post-resurrection Christ, light, pleasurable, and pleasing to nature. This is the best condition, says natural man, because he thinks it is best for *him*. (124) [emphasis is in the original text]

But true discipleship means sharing in the cross of Christ by imitating Him.

All that has been written here Christ taught throughout His life of thirty-three and a half years, long in comparison with the brevity of these words: "Follow me." It is a brief word but if you are to follow Him you must surrender all things, just as everything was surrendered in Him, so completely that no other creature has done the like of it, or will ever do.

Furthermore, if you wish to follow Him you must take the cross upon you. The cross is the same as the Christ life and that is a bitter cross for natural man. Christ says about the cross: He who does not leave all and does not take the cross upon himself is not worthy of Me and is not My disciple and follows Me not. (143)

***

In what remains of this meditation, we will study one last important text in which the Frankfurt Priest further describes the cross-shaped life of Christ's disciples. For the purposes of analysis, we will divide the text into two segments. We will hear how he compares and contrasts the false discipleship of Christians who claim they have completely triumphed over suffering with the true discipleship of those Christians who joyfully imitate in their own lives the life of their crucified Lord:

Wherever such a divinized person lives, there we have the best, noblest, and, in God's eyes, most valuable life that ever was or can be. Attachment to this kind of life is rooted in a love of goodness for the sake of the good. It has an eye for the best and noblest in all things for the sake of the good. And it is so deep that it can never be quite abandoned and rejected.

In the case of divine sorrow, the kind we now have described, the person who harbors it cannot possibly get out of its thrall even if he should live to the latter day. [emphasis added]

Should you die a thousand deaths and be afflicted by all the misfortunes that might ever befall, you would rather suffer than abandon the noble life. If given an opportunity to exchange your life for that of an angel's, you would not take it. (III)

These sober reflections are immediately followed in the text by a teaching that seems to speak directly to us who live in the cultural setting of modern-day America. Pragmatism and utilitarianism are in his cross-hairs. He bluntly declares that all those who become Christians thinking that they will gain some practical use of it are sadly mistaken. Such utilitarianism denies cross-shaped discipleship. The Frankfurt Priest implies that such triumphalism has the smell of death about it because those who practice it do not possess Christ's life, and Christ's life is salvation. His teachings on the matter could not be clearer:

> We have now answered the question: When man can obtain nothing in addition to what he has by virtue of the Christ life and does not seem to have much practical use for it, what further meaning does it have?
>
> *The life in Christ is not chosen because one derives use from it or can obtain something thereby but on account of love for its nobility and because it is dear to God and highly rated by Him.* [emphasis added]
>
> Whoever says he has had enough of it or that he wants to put it aside has never tasted it or come to know it from within. For the person who has in truth felt it or tasted it can never give it up. Therefore, the person who leads a life in Christ with the intention of obtaining some use or earning some glory from it embraces this life as a hireling who is out for recompense and not from above; he possesses none of Christ's life. He who is not devoted to it out of love has no part of it. He might fancy he has it but he is mistaken. Christ led His life not

from expectation of reward but from love. And love makes life light, not heavy, so that it is joyfully led and willingly endured.

But he who does not lead his life from love but fancies it should bring reward, for him the eternal life turns so heavy that he wishes to be promptly rid of it. It is a sign of a hireling that he wishes his work would soon end. But a true lover in Christ does not take offense at life's work, length, or suffering. (111-112)

***

Having retrieved the Frankfurt Priest's rich insights into the imitation of Christ, some general conclusions may now be drawn. The goal that is to be reached by the imitation of Christ is that which the Frankfurt Priest calls our "true end." This goal can only be obtained by faith because as yet "no one knows how to say anything about what the true end is. Yet, he who would like to know may he walk the right path toward it, namely, Christ's life." (89) The Christian trusts that it is enough to know that the imitation of Christ and His cruciform life does lead to the goal. This is not arm-chair theology. It is wisdom and discernment won by the blood of the Apostles and the martyrs. Paul Gavrilyuk has said:

> "[In the early church] the theology of martyrdom very quickly linked the idea of imitation to that of participation in the passion of Christ...If communion in Christ's suffering is open to those who follow him, then Christ's suffering itself must be in some sense an enduring reality, extending beyond the boundaries of his earthly ministry."[37]

Christ invites everyone to die to self in order to be reborn into a life that imitates Him. The structure of Christian existence that is given shape by the imitation of Christ is summed up by Hans Urs von Balthasar in the form of two syllogisms:

Only through the experience of suffering does man acquire true knowledge of God and of himself. Christ, moreover, is true man. Therefore, he too acquires knowledge of God and man through the experience of suffering.

Christ is exemplary man, also in his experience. Christ's exemplary experience becomes a law for whoever follows after him. Therefore, when he comes to know God and himself through the experience of suffering, the follower of Christ experiences something of Christ's own experience.[38]

Life in Christ is the living out of a life that mirrors the cross of Christ. Love is not only rejected by the world, it is rewarded with persecution. The believer's goal is to be able to say with Paul, "I have been crucified with Christ; it is no longer I who live, but Christ who lives in me." (Gal 2:20) At bottom, this is not a statement about the human capacity for change, as though human beings had something to boast about. It is a statement about God, and about God's desire to transform us in and through Christ. However, given the revelation of God's desire to transform us in Christ, the following statement of John Paul II at the closing Mass at the World Youth Gathering in Toronto in 2002 is also true: "We are not the sum of our weaknesses and failures. We are the sum of the Father's love for us, and our capacity to become the image of his Son." In a similar vein, Jesus' exhortation "Be perfect, therefore, as your heavenly Father is perfect" (Mat 5:48) is in fact a promise full of grace. The good news of the Kingdom is not adequately conveyed by such language as "God loves you" and "God loves you just the way you are." While certainly true, God has higher expectations and greater plans for us than such words suggest. The vocation of believers does not consist in resting contentedly upon the status quo. Rather, believers hear in God's call an invitation to a life of growth in grace. God wishes to transform us.

MEDITATION IV

THE WAY OF IMITATION

Eternal Wisdom: "No one can reach the heights of the divinity or unusual sweetness without first being drawn through the bitterness I experienced as man. The higher one climbs without sharing the paths of my humanity, the deeper one falls. My humanity is the path one takes; my suffering is the gate through which one must pass who will come to what you are seeking." — Henry Suso

IN THIS MEDITATION WE learn that discipleship to Jesus Christ, far from encouraging the avoidance of suffering, involves a progressive conformation to God that can only be attained through the imitation of Christ and His way of the cross. The form of sin that reflects the all-too-human refusal to follow Christ in suffering may be given the name *acedia*. *Acedia* has to do with a human being's refusal to accept his rightful place in the world. To suffer from *acedia* means, as Josef Pieper has said, "that the human being has given up on the very responsibility that comes with his dignity: that he does not want to be what God wants him to be, and that means that he does not want to be what he really, and in the ultimate sense *is*..."[39] [emphasis in text] In this fourth meditation Henry Suso teaches us about how God overcomes *acedia*, drawing human beings into a redemptive participation in the divine love of the Trinity. In the following statement

Wolfhart Pannenberg frames our discussion as he speaks eloquently of this participation, this cross-shaped discipleship, which is made possible by the self-emptying of the Son of God:

> The self-emptying and self-humbling of the Son that found perfect expression in the history of Jesus Christ should not be understood first as an unselfish turning to us, though it is that also. Rather, it is primarily an expression of the self-giving of the Son to the Father in an obedience that desires nothing for self but serves totally the glorifying of God in the coming of his kingdom. Precisely thus the way of the Son is also an expression of the love of God for us. For by the self-distinction of the Son from the Father, God draws near to us. The *kenosis* of the Son serves the drawing near of the Father. It is thus an expression of the divine love, for we attain to our salvation in the closeness of God to us and in our participation in his life.[40] [emphasis in text]

***

In his *Little Book of Eternal Wisdom*, Henry Suso[41] traces the Christian path that leads a person to make one of the most important decisions of his life, namely, to resolve to imitate Christ.[42] The book presents a lively dialogue between eternal Wisdom and a servant-disciple. In a series of teachings and prophecies—that Suso testifies as having come to him directly from the living Christ—Wisdom teaches the servant about the role of suffering in the life of faith. The servant figure is in fact Suso himself, so the book can be read as a personal memoir of faith. We begin this meditation with a study of this powerful little book, and follow it up with an analysis of his even more personal book, *The Life of the Servant*. Both of these books put on display his narrative style of theologizing that makes his work accessible and thought provoking.

In the opening pages of *Little Book of Eternal Wisdom* Suso recounts how God slowly drew His servant-disciple (that is, Suso himself) to God's self. He writes:

> These are words written in the Book of Wisdom [8:2] and refer to beautiful, lovely eternal Wisdom…"I have loved her and sought her out from my youth and have chosen her for my bride."
>
> An undisciplined spirit, as it first ventured forth, strayed onto the paths of error. There, eternal Wisdom in an indescribable spiritual form confronted him and drew him by means of both pleasant and unpleasant until it brought him to the right path of divine truth. And, when he reflected deeply on how wondrously he had been drawn, he addressed God thus: "Dear gentle Lord, since I was a child, my spirit has been searching with unslaked thirst for something. And what this was, Lord, I have never yet fully grasped. For many a year, Lord, I have pursued it feverishly, yet could never attain it because I never really knew what it was; and yet it is something that draws my heart and soul to itself and without which I cannot ever really find peace. Lord, in the early days of my childhood I would search for it as I saw others do before me—in creatures. And the more I sought, the less I found; and the closer I came, the farther away I got. Concerning every form that I looked at I heard an inner voice, and before I would occupy myself with it completely or devote myself to it in peace, it would say: 'This is not what you are searching for.' Always I have had this force driving me away from all things. Lord, my heart is raging to possess it because it wants it. It certainly has more than once sensed what it is *not*, Lord; but it is still uninstructed about what it *is*. [Italics in text] Alas, beloved Lord of heaven…what is the nature of that which so mysteriously moves within me?"

> Response of *eternal Wisdom*: Don't you recognize it? It has, after all, lovingly embraced you and has often stood in your path until it gained you for itself alone.
>
> The *servant*: Lord, I never saw or heard it at all. I don't

know what it is.

Response of *eternal Wisdom*: That is not surprising. It was caused by your intimacy with creatures and your unfamiliarity with it. But now open your inner eyes and see who I am. It is I, eternal Wisdom, who chose you for myself in eternity with the embrace of my eternal providence. I have blocked your path whenever you would have been separated from me if I had let you be. You always found something repugnant in all things. This is the surest mark of my chosen ones, that I want them for myself.

The *servant*: Tender loving Wisdom, is it you that I have been so long searching for? Are you what my spirit has ever and again struggled to attain? O God, why have you waited so long to reveal yourself to me? How very long you put it off! How many a wearisome way have I plodded!

Response of *eternal Wisdom*: If I had acted earlier, you would not have recognized the value of my treasures as intensely as you do now. (211-212)

Having told the story about how God slowly drew him to God's goodness, Henry Suso turns to God out of great joy and asks God to complete His work in him. Suso states that his heart wants to live "all its days with you in constant love and full praise":

The *servant:* O infinite Good, how sweetly have you now poured out your goodness in me! When I did not exist, you gave me being. When I left you, you would not leave me. When I tried to escape you, you so gently took me captive. O eternal Wisdom, my heart would now like to burst into a thousand pieces and, embracing you in its bliss, consume all its days with you in constant love and full praise. This is the desire of my heart. That person is truly blessed whose desire you so lovingly anticipate that you never let him rest until he seeks his rest in you alone!

O exquisite, lovely Wisdom, since I have found it is you

whom my soul loves, do not despise your poor creature. Look how numb my heart is to the whole world, in joy and sorrow. Lord, is my heart ever to remain mute to you? Permit, beloved Lord, permit my wretched soul to speak a word with you, for my fully laden heart can no longer carry on alone. It has no one in this wide world with whom to share its burden except you, tender, beloved Lord and Brother. Lord, you alone see and know the nature of a heart filled with love. You know that no one can love something he cannot at all know. Therefore, since I shall now love you alone, let me get to know you better so that I can learn to love you completely. (212-213)

The tenor of these words betrays the fact that the servant does not yet know what true discipleship with Christ entails. Eternal Wisdom directs Suso into a dialogue that leads inexorably to the declaration that discipleship entails participation in Christ's bitter suffering:

Response of *eternal Wisdom*: According to the order of nature, the loftiest flowing forth of all beings from their primal origin proceeds from the highest beings to the lowest; but the return to the origin proceeds from the lowest beings to the highest. And so, if you want to see me in my uncreated Godhead, you should learn to know and love me here in my suffering humanity. This is the quickest way to eternal happiness.

The *servant*: Lord, I shall remind you today of the boundless love that brought you down from your lofty throne, from the royal abode in the heart of the Father, into exile and misery for thirty-three years. And this love you had for me and for all men you show most clearly in that most bitter suffering of your brutal death. Lord, be mindful of this: that you revealed yourself to my soul in the most lovely spiritual form that your immense love ever assumed.

Response of *eternal Wisdom*: *The more exhausted, the closer to death from love I am, the more lovely I am to a well-ordered spirit.* [emphasis added] My boundless love reveals itself in the deep bitterness of my suffering just as the sun reveals itself in its splendor, as the rose does in its fragrance, and as fire does in its searing heat. And so listen attentively to how intense was the suffering on your behalf.

After the Last Supper, when on the mountain I surrendered myself to the throes of a cruel death and discovered that I was about to confront it, because of the fear in my gentle heart and the distress of my whole human body, a bloody sweat began to pour out of me. I was treacherously taken captive, tightly bound and led off to agony. All through the night I was shamefully mistreated with blows, spat upon and blindfolded. In the morning, before Caiaphas, I was slandered and condemned to death. One could see the indestructible heartbreak of my pure Mother from the time she first saw me in distress until I was executed on the cross. I was brought before Pilate ignominiously, falsely accused and condemned to death. With their cruel eyes they stood opposite me, powerful as giants, and I stood before them like a gentle lamb. I, eternal Wisdom, was scorned as a fool in white garments before Herod. My fair body was painfully torn open and marred by the wanton blows of the scourge. My gentle head was pierced and my loving countenance dripped with blood and spit. Thus was I condemned in misery and shamefully led forth with my cross to death. They screamed at me so cruelly that the air rang with their cries: "Crucify him! Crucify the evil fiend!" (213-214)

In response to this vivid account of Christ's sufferings, the servant becomes confused and alarmed. In so doing he demonstrates that he has failed to discern the full meaning of the words spoken by Eternal Wisdom: "The more exhausted, the closer to death from love I am, the more lovely I am to a well-ordered spirit." The servant is not yet able to behold this strange beauty. In his response he instead questions God's ways by saying:

The *servant*: O Lord, the beginning is so completely terrible.

How will it end? If I were to see a wild animal thus treated before my eyes, I could scarcely endure it. How right it is that your suffering pass through my heart and soul! But, Lord, my heart is greatly confused. Beloved Lord, I seek always your divinity, but you show me your humanity. I seek your sweetness, but you stress what is bitter. I wish always to suckle, but you teach me to struggle. O Lord, why are you doing this? (214)

The servant admits to Wisdom that in his search for God he desires to find God's sweetness, hoping to follow that sweetness down the path that leads to the Lord's divinity. The servant must instead learn the harsh lesson that the path to divinity runs through a life that shares in Christ's suffering humanity. To follow Christ, to have a share in His life, means to share in His suffering. The imitation of Christ, a form of striving for perfect self-surrender to the Lordship of the Crucified One, is another way to suffer well in union with God.

In the next several exchanges, the servant experiences great difficulty accepting the role that suffering must play in discipleship. Eternal Wisdom has to help him think this issue through before the servant will be willing to say yes to suffering. There is no equivocation; suffering is the gate that leads to new life:

> Response of *eternal Wisdom*: *No one can reach the heights of the divinity or unusual sweetness without first being drawn through the bitterness I experienced as man. The higher one climbs without sharing the paths of my humanity, the deeper one falls. My humanity is the path one takes; my suffering is the gate through which one must pass who will come to what you are seeking.* [emphasis added] And so, away with faint-heartedness and enter with me the lists of knightly steadfastness. Indulgence is not fitting for the servant when the lord is practicing warlike boldness. I shall clothe you with my armor because all my suffering has to be endured by you as far as you are able...(214)
>
> The *servant*: O Lord, this will be a dreadful path for me! My whole being shudders at these words, Lord, say something.

In your eternal wisdom could you find no other way to keep me and show me your love? Could you not spare yourself this great suffering and spare me having to share this bitter suffering? How very strange your judgments seem! (215)

The servant questions the necessity of Christ's suffering. In reply, Wisdom Personified explains that it was due to the "improper pleasures" of humankind that people "lost eternal joy," so God had to suffer in order to reveal His infinite love to humankind:

Response of *eternal Wisdom*: No one should try to probe the unfathomable abyss of my mysterious being, in which I ordain all things in my eternal foreknowledge. No one can grasp it. Here, both this and many other things were a possibility, and yet they will never happen. Still, you should know that in the present order that has flowed out (from God) there can be no better way. The Lord of nature does not consider what he can accomplish in nature. Rather, he looks to what is most fitting for each individual creature and acts accordingly.

How, then, can a person better know the mysteries of God than in the humanity he assumed? How can a person who because of improper pleasures lost eternal joy be more properly instructed about this joy? How could the untried path of an austere and scorned way of life be better traveled than that it be traveled by God himself? If you had been condemned to death and someone allowed himself to be executed in your place, how could he show you more faithfulness and love, or better move you to love him in return? If my infinite love, my indescribable mercy, my shining Godhead, my congenial humanity, my brotherly devotion and my intimate love cannot move someone to intense love, what could then soften a stone-hearted heart?...

...*Do not be afraid to follow me in suffering. He who possesses God so intimately that suffering becomes easy has no reason to complain. No one has more benefit from my extraordinary sweetness than those who stand with me in deepest bitterness. No one complains more about the bitterness of the husk than he who has not experienced the inner sweetness of the kernel. The battle is half won if you have an able companion.* [emphasis added] (215-216)

The servant is confused as to why God should ask him to follow in the footsteps of the crucified Son of God and suggests that there must be a better way. Eternal Wisdom responds: Only the Crucified One can show lost humankind the way back to God. Wisdom hints that the servant is not alone: "The battle is half won if you have an able companion." The "able companion" of which he speaks is Jesus Christ! In point of fact, being with Christ and in Christ makes all of the difference for the sufferer. As the significance of this spiritual reality of union with Christ dawns upon the servant, there arises within him a sincere desire to represent all loving hearts as he mourns over the suffering and death of Jesus:

> O dear Lord, your suffering affects some hearts very deeply; they can lament for you earnestly and weep for you sincerely. O God, if only I knew how and were able to represent all loving hearts in my lamenting! If I could only shed the radiant tears of all eyes and speak the words of grief of all tongues, then I would show you now how deeply your pitiable anguish moves me! (217)

The servant becomes absorbed with a concern to mourn the sufferings of Christ. But Eternal Wisdom corrects him, saying that it is better for him to imitate Christ's exemplary life in his deeds, rather than for him to weep over Christ's sufferings on the cross:

> Response of *eternal Wisdom*: No one shows better how deeply my suffering affects him than he who bears it with me through the evidence of deeds. I prefer a free heart, untroubled by any transitory love, that pursues perfection through

constant efforts by imitating my exemplary life rather than
that you should constantly mourn for me and weep as many
tears in grieving for my torment as there are drops of water
that ever fell from the skies. That it be imitated was the reason
why I endured my bitter death, however dear and touching I
may find such tears. (217)

In response to this the servant decides to devote himself to the
imitation of Christ:

> The *servant*: O gentle Lord, since a loving imitation of your
> meek way of life and your suffering from love is so very pleas-
> ing to you, I shall spend all my efforts from now on to imi-
> tate you joyfully rather than to lament with weeping, though I
> should do both according to your words. And so teach me how
> to become like you in this suffering. (217)

Eternal Wisdom then teaches the servant how to begin to imitate
Christ:

> Response of *eternal Wisdom*: Break off your pleasure in
> looking at wantonness and in hearing frivolous things. In your
> love (for me) find pleasure and enjoyment in those things that
> you used to find repugnant. For my sake give up pampering
> your body. You should seek all your rest in me, should love
> bodily discomfort, should willingly endure evil from others,
> should desire humiliation, and should diminish your desires
> and kill all your pleasures. In the school of wisdom this is the
> beginning that one reads from the open, outstretched book of
> my crucified body. (217)

Yet, after Wisdom's extensive exhortation to the servant about the
imitation of Christ and its centrality to a life devoted to God, he
abruptly includes this caveat:

But consider! If a person does all that he can, still—is there anyone in this world who is for me what I am for him? (217)

Eternal Wisdom, Christ himself, directs this question to the servant, thereby putting a limit upon what can be accomplished by those who imitate Him. By asking this rhetorical question, Christ is simultaneously affirming the act of imitation even as He puts it in its proper place. This question from Wisdom carries within it a fundamental insight: Since Jesus is the God-Man, any imitation of Him on the part of His followers can only be accomplished through cooperation with the Spirit of Christ that is at work in them.

***

Having considered Suso's *Little Book of Eternal Wisdom,* we turn now to his most popular book, *Life of the Servant.* Written in Middle High German in beautiful and clear narrative prose, it was one of the most beloved devotional books in medieval Germany. In the opening pages, Suso has this to say about the circumstances around which the book was written:

There was a Friar Preacher in Germany, a Swabian by birth. May his name be written in the book of life. He had a longing to become and be called a servant of eternal Wisdom. He became acquainted with a holy enlightened person [Dominican nun Elsbeth Stagel] who was beset with hardship and suffering in this world. This person asked of him that he tell her from his own experience something about his sufferings so that her own stricken heart might take strength from it, and she kept after him for a long time. When he would visit her, she would draw him out with personal questions about his beginnings and progress, about some of his practices and the sufferings he had experienced. He told her about these things in spiritual confidence. Because she found comfort and guidance in these things, she wrote it all down as a help for herself and for others as well…(63)

In one of the book's chapters, Suso presents an unforgettable meditation on the topic, "How a Person Should Offer Up His Sufferings to God." (Chapter 31) Because it is so important, it is presented here in its entirety. Suso was able to teach theological truths in narrative form. Unlike Meister Eckhart, who wrote in densely philosophical terminology, Henry Suso sought to reach a wide readership. As a result he expressed his teachings didactically through the use of carefully formulated personal anecdotes. In order to highlight the five major themes that Suso discusses in this chapter, it is divided into five segments here.

First, the servant prays for patience in suffering that truly praises God. Just before this section of his book, Suso describes how on one occasion he suffered so severely that he was near death. During this time of testing, he sought God's guidance on how he might learn patience in suffering. Closely related to this was his keen desire to offer up his afflictions to God as a way to praise Him:

> Once when the suffering servant thought over this grueling struggle in deep contemplation and discovered also God's hidden marvels therein, he turned to God with a deep sigh and said, "O gentle Lord, these sufferings just described can be viewed externally as sharp thorns that pierce flesh and bone. Therefore, gentle Lord, besides the sharp thorns of suffering, let some sweet fruit of good teaching spring forth so that we poor struggling men might bear our suffering with more patience and can better offer up our afflictions for the praise of God." (126)

Second, God answers the servant's prayer when "something spoke sweetly within him." Suso was a student of Eckhart for a time. He was also a friend and colleague of his fellow Dominican, Johannes Tauler, with whom he shared duties as leaders of the Friends of God lay movement. In this second segment from Chapter 31, Suso demonstrates his ability to convey insights that came to him out of his mystical experience in a way that is understandable to a lay person.

Suso describes how God gave him the gifts of patience in suffering and a joyful determination to offer praise and thanksgiving to God on behalf of all those who suffer. Notice how a concern for his personal suffering widens to include a tender compassion for others:

> After he had been seeking this from God for quite some time, it happened that he was transported into himself and beyond himself. And in a state of withdrawal from his senses something spoke sweetly within him thus: "I want to show you the lofty nobility of my suffering and how a man in his suffering should offer up his afflictions in a praiseworthy manner to his dear God."
>
> At these sweet words spoken within him his soul dissolved in his body and, with his senses absent, out of the unfathomable fullness of his heart, the arms of his soul somehow stretched forth to the far ends of the world in heaven and on earth. Thanking and praising God with immense longing in his heart, he said:
>
> "Lord, up till now I have praised you in my writings, using everything in creatures that can be delightful and attractive. But now I must burst forth joyfully in a new song of unusual praise that I have hitherto not known but have now become familiar with in this suffering. This is how it is: I desire from the boundless abyss of my heart that all the sufferings and grief that I have ever experienced, and, in addition, the painful suffering of all hearts, the pains of all wounds, the groans of all the sick, the sighs of all sad people, the tears of all weeping eyes, the insults suffered by all those oppressed, the needs of all poor indigent widows and orphans, the dire wants of all the thirsty and hungry, the blood spilled by all the martyrs, the breaking of their selfish wills by all the joyful and blossoming youth, the painful practices of all the friends of God, and all the hidden and open suffering and sorrow that I or any other

afflicted person ever experienced with regard to their bodies, possessions, reputation, friends and relatives, or depression, or whatever any man shall suffer up to the last day—I desire that all this may praise you eternally, heavenly Father, and honor your only-begotten Son from eternity to eternity. *And I, your poor servant, desire to be today the devoted substitute for all suffering people who do not know how to bear their suffering in patient and thankful praise of God, so that I might offer up to you in their place today their sufferings, however they may have suffered.* [emphasis added] I offer it to you in their stead, just as if I myself alone had suffered it all physically and in my heart as I desired. And I present it today in their place to your only-begotten Son, that he may be praised by it forever and those suffering may be consoled, whether they are still in this vale of lamentation or in the other world in your power." (126-127)

Here Suso describes an instance of the transformative work of God's Spirit in the soul. This text is an expression of the expansive action of divine love in the human heart. We are shown how what had begun for Henry Suso as a simple personal desire to find patience in suffering is, by the grace of God, transformed into a prayerful longing to secure this patience for the whole human race. The servant is imitating Christ by letting Christ's sacrificial love work in and through him for the benefit of all.

Third, "For love makes love like itself and inclines itself to love wherever at all it can." Suso exhorts:

Oh, all you people suffering with me, look at me and listen to what I tell you. We poor members should console ourselves and rejoice in our noble Head; that is, in the beloved only-begotten Son who went before us in suffering and on earth never experienced a day without it. Note well, if in a poor family there were only one rich and respected man, the whole family would rejoice because of him. O worthy Head of all us members, be merciful to us and, where we lack true patience in any adversity arising from human weakness, make this good for us to your dear heavenly Father! Remember that you once came to help one of your servants. As he was about to turn cowardly in suffering, you said to him, 'Take courage and look at me. I was noble and poor. I was gentle and miserable, born from all joys and yet full of suffering.' Hence we, the seasoned knights of the imperial Lord, do not turn cowardly; the noble followers of our respected leader, we take courage and are not unhappy to suffer. For if there were no other advantage or good thing in suffering except that we become much more like Christ, our fair and shining model, it would be well worth it. One thing seems true to me: *If after this life God wanted to reward equally those who had suffered and those who had not, then certainly we should still choose suffering just because it makes us like Christ. For love makes love like itself and inclines itself to love wherever at all it can.* [emphasis added] (127-128)

Christ is "our fair and shining model." Suso argues that the mere fact that suffering conforms us to Christ makes the suffering worthwhile. Then, he delivers a beautifully formulated summary statement: "For love makes love like itself and inclines itself to love wherever at all it can." Divine love is central to everything we do, even in our suffering.

Fourth, consider the question: "What boldness allows us to dare to presume that our suffering makes us like you, noble Lord? Answer: "In your mighty power all dissimilarity is put aside."

Let us revisit the question that Christ asked His servant, which we discussed earlier in our meditation on Suso's *Little Book of Eternal Wisdom*: "If a person does all that he can, still—is there anyone in this world who is for me what I am for him?" (217) The meaning of Christ's words is now clear: the Christian does not earn salvation through the imitation of Christ; rather it is God, in and through Christ, who redeems and transforms the sinner into an ever closer likeness to Christ. (II Cor 3:18) The Catechism puts it just right: "It is impossible to keep the Lord's commandment by imitating the divine model from outside; there has to be a vital participation, coming from the depths of the heart, in the holiness and the mercy and the love of our God. Only the Spirit by whom we live can make "ours" the same mind that was in Christ Jesus."[43] Suso's way of saying this is: "In your almighty power all dissimilarity is put aside."[44] He remarks:

> "But what boldness allows us dare to presume that our suffering makes us like you, noble Lord? Alas, [your] suffering and [our] suffering—how completely unlike (each other) you are! Lord, Lord, you alone are the one who suffered without reason or guilt. But who can claim that he never gave cause for suffering? If he is without guilt regarding his present suffering, then he has reason to do penance because of something else. Therefore, all of us who have ever suffered, let us all sit down in a gigantic circle all around. And you, gentle, intimate, innocent Beloved, sit down in our midst in this circle of suffering people. Our thirsting interiors shall burst wide open out of deep desire for you. O Fountain of grace rushing forth. Behold a marvel! The earth that is most marked by drought absorbs the storm-floods of rain. And the more guilty we weak men have become, the more we embrace you within us in our wounded hearts and want you, as your divine mouth itself has said: in joy or in sorrow, washed in your painful bleeding wounds and made innocent of all evil in all things—because of this you shall have eternal praise and honor from us, and we shall receive grace from you, *for in your mighty power all dissimilarity is put aside.*" [emphasis added]
>
> After the servant had sat there very quietly for a good while until all this became clear in the innermost part of his soul with great intensity, he got up in good spirits and thanked God for his grace. (128)

Fifth, in the final paragraphs of Chapter 31, Suso describes the three divine gifts that are given to those who in faith pass through the gate of Christ's suffering humanity. He explains how these gifts—the

---

gifts of wishing, peace of mind, and union with God—are given to those who enjoy mystical union with God:

> Once, on a joyous Easter Day...the servant...asked God to tell him what people receive on earth who for his sake have undergone much suffering. And in a state of contemplation this enlightenment came from God: "Rejoice in your hearts, all you suffering forsaken men, for your patience shall be highly praised... Three special gifts I shall give them which are so precious that no one can estimate their value. (129)

> The first is that I shall give them the power of wishing in heaven and on earth so that everything they ever wish for comes true....People who are successful in the breakthrough, which one must anticipate by withdrawing from oneself and all things—not many succeed—such people's minds and hearts are so completely lost in God that they somehow have no consciousness of self except by perceiving self and all things in their first origin. Therefore, they take great pleasure and enjoyment from anything that God does, as though God had nothing to do with it and had turned it over to them to deal with as they saw fit. Thus they have attained within themselves the power of wishing. (129-130)

Suso's point is that when the will of a sufferer is in conformity with God's, whatever he wishes for will come true, precisely because his wish coincides with God's will. The sufferer lives the prayer: "Not my will, but Thy will be done."

> Second, I shall grant them my divine peace that neither angels nor devils nor men nor any other creature can take from them....Heaven and earth serve them, and all creatures are obedient to them in the sense that everything does what it does or leaves undone what it leaves undone. Such people feel no sadness in their hearts regarding anything, because sorrow

and suffering in one's heart happens only if one's will, after carefully considering the matter, would want to be released from it. Externally, such people do indeed feel pleasure and pain like other people, and it affects them even more than others because of their refined spirit of gentleness. However, there is no place for it to remain within them. Outwardly, they remain steadfast in turmoil. Because they have withdrawn from self, they are lifted up, as far as this is possible, so that their joy is whole and constant in all things. For in the divine being, where their hearts have lost themselves, there is no place for suffering or sadness, but only for peace and joy. (129-130)

God grants to the sufferer divine peace that keeps sorrow and suffering from penetrating into his heart and soul, although he does continue to feel both pleasure and pain externally.

> Third, *I shall kiss them so intimately and embrace them so lovingly that I am they and they are me, and we two shall remain a single one forever and ever.* [emphasis added] And since long waiting causes pain to restless hearts, this joy shall not be put off at the present time for a single moment. It shall begin now and be enjoyed eternally to the degree that mortal men, each according to his capacity, can bear more or less of it. (129)

Sufferers are united with God here and now and enjoy a loving embrace with God. This embrace is so intimate that God can say of these sufferers, "I am they and they are me."

MEDITATION V

THE WAY OF CO-SUFFERING

"Compassion is a wounding of the heart which love extends to all without distinction. This wound cannot be healed as long as anyone still suffers, for to compassion alone, above all other virtues, God has commended sorrow and suffering. For this reason Christ says:"Blessed are the sorrowing, for they shall be consoled." (Mt 5:4) That will take place when they reap in joy what they now, through compassion and sympathy, sow in sorrow." — John Ruusbroec[45]

WHEN I FIRST READ this remarkable teaching on compassion, the words immediately hit home because they simply and clearly confirmed for me a belief that I had long held about the vital role of compassion in Christian life. Even as a child I thought that I had no right to ever forget the suffering of others. In our church sanctuary we had a stained glass window that depicted Jesus in the Garden of Gethsemane. In the background were the three disciples of Jesus who had fallen asleep, unable to watch with Christ one hour. They had forgotten. Romano Guardini has spoken eloquently of the failure of Peter, John, and Andrew (who surely represent the entire human race) to watch with Jesus as He prayed, accepting the will of the Father that He suffer and die. Guardini says, "In the face of such infinite suffering, their little capacity for compassion must have rebounded like the heart of a small child when the grown-ups are engulfed in some shattering experience: it turns aside, begins to play, or simply falls asleep."[46] If this be so, how can we square this call from God to remember all who suffer with this human failure to do so?

In this meditation we hear Ruusbroec's answer: God puts the desire to show compassion within us as a fruit of Christ's loving presence in our souls. It is *God's love and compassion in us* that prompts us to desire to become instruments of love for those who suffer. And others can extend the same compassion to us in our sufferings as well. It is God who knows our sufferings and remembers them. God never forgets. Believers can participate in God's compassion.

***

Here is Ruusbroec's full statement on compassion from *The Spiritual Espousals*:

> This kindness gives rise to compassion and to a general sympathy with everyone, for only a kind person can share the sorrows of all others. This compassion is an interior movement of a heart filled with pity for the material and spiritual needs of all persons. Compassion makes a person suffer with Christ in his passion as one considers all that it entailed....Compassion also makes a person look to himself and recognize his faults and failings in the practice of virtue and the worship of God, his lukewarmness and laziness, the multiplicity of his failings, the way he has wasted time and the way he presently falls short in the practice of virtues and a perfect way of life. This makes a person have pity on himself in true compassion.
>
> Compassion likewise makes a person aware of the way others have erred and gone astray: their negligence of God and of their eternal salvation, their ingratitude for all the good that God has done for them and all the sufferings that he endured for them....
>
> A person should also observe with pity the bodily needs

of his neighbor and the manifold sufferings of human nature: hunger, thirst, cold, nakedness, sickness, poverty, scorn, the oppression of the poor in so many ways, the grief caused by the loss of relatives, friends, possessions, honor, and peace, and the countless afflictions which weigh upon human nature. All this moves a good person to compassion and makes him suffer with all others. But such a person suffers most of all because people are so impatient in their sufferings and thereby lose their reward, often to the point of even deserving hell. Such is the work of compassion and pity.

This work of compassion and of a love common to all overcomes and drives away the third capital sin, which is hatred or envy, *for compassion is a wounding of the heart which love extends to all without distinction. This wound cannot be healed as long as anyone still suffers, for to compassion alone, above all other virtues, God has commended sorrow and suffering. For this reason Christ says, "Blessed are the sorrowing, for they shall be consoled." (Mt 5:4) That will take place when they reap in joy what they now, through compassion and sympathy, sow in sorrow.* [emphasis added][47]

This statement, especially the last paragraph, deserves an extended meditation.

First: "Compassion is a wounding of the heart…"

As the light of God's love in Christ strikes the soul, God's Spirit begins to impress upon the human heart an ever-deepening awareness of the depths of God's loving compassion. The world is seen with new eyes, the eyes of faith. This light of love—this compassion that knows no bounds—causes the wound of love. Love and woundedness must go hand in hand under the conditions of a world that is estranged from God. Think: the cross. Having been created in the image of God, human beings possess the potential to serve as agents of God's compassion. But actualizing this potential comes at a price.

The stringent demands of sacrificial love are an intrinsic part of discipleship to Jesus Christ. Following Christ means being open to the possibility of suffering irremediable scarring. Vulnerability to suffering is a necessary condition of being able to love at all. C.S. Lewis notes that those who do not dare to love will suffer a living death:

> To love at all is to be vulnerable. Love anything, and your heart will certainly be wrung and possibly be broken. If you want to make sure of keeping it intact, you must give your heart to no one, not even to an animal. Wrap it carefully round with hobbies and little luxuries; avoid all entanglements; lock it up safe in the casket or coffin of your selfishness. But in that casket—safe, dark, motionless, airless—it will change. It will not be broken; it will become unbreakable, impenetrable, irremediable.[48]

There are many forms of death; a loveless life is a living death. From the Christian perspective comes a recognition of the certainty that every human being will suffer. The cross teaches us that much. The Gospel reveals that the crucial question that is addressed to each individual person, as a being created in the image of God, is: Will you suffer alone—in the absence of any faith in a loving God—or in communion with the Crucified One and His Church?

Second: "…which love extends to all without distinction"

The Medieval Church used the Latin term *misericordia* to refer to the loving communal response to the harsh and traumatic scarring that all too often afflicts human beings. This term denoted "grief or sorrow over someone else's distress…just insofar as one understands the other's distress as one's own. One may do this because of some pre-existing tie to the other—the other is already one's friend or kin—or because in understanding the other's distress one recognizes that it could instead have been one's own."[49] *Misericordia* is a misery-of-the-heart that issues forth in acts of love inside a communal group or family.

As indispensable as *misericordia* is to the life of a community, the role that compassion plays is even more important because of its reach beyond the local community. Again Ruusbroec: "Compassion is a wounding of the heart that love extends to all without distinction." Graham Greene illustrates the radical call to love *all* in one of his novels:

> He went down on his knees and pulled [his daughter] to him, while she giggled and struggled to be free: 'I love you. I am your father and I love you. Try to understand that.' He held her tightly by the wrist and suddenly she stayed still, looking up at him. He said, 'I would give my life, that's nothing, my soul...my dear, try to understand that you are—important.' That was the difference, he had always known, between his faith and theirs, the political leaders of the people who cared only for things like the state, the republic: this child was more important than a whole continent. He said, 'You must take care of yourself because you are so—necessary...' He said, 'Good-bye, my dear,' and clumsily kissed her—a silly infatuated ageing man, who as soon as he released her and started padding back to the plaza could feel behind his hunched shoulders the whole vile world coming round the child to ruin her... One mustn't have human affections—or rather one must love every soul as if it were one's own child. The passion to protect must extend itself over a world...⁵⁰

Greene expresses the truth of the boundlessness of love and in so doing hints at the beloved Scripture verse that encapsulates the Gospel: "For God so loved *the world* that he gave his only Son." Divine love embraces all things, right down to the solitary individual. Similarly, Maximus the Confessor notes, "So the man whose will has become good and free loves all men equally, the just for their nature and their good will, sinners for their nature and with the compassionate pity which is felt for a madman who escapes into the night."⁵¹

Third: "This wound cannot be healed as long as anyone still suffers, for to compassion alone, above all other virtues, God has commended sorrow and suffering."

Jacques Barzum once commented that Abraham Lincoln was a man whose "morbid regard for truth and abnormal suppression of aggressive impulses suggest that he hugged a secret wound."[52] Lincoln apparently went to his grave with this wound. In a therapeutic age such as ours, there is a desire to downplay the deep and traumatic wounds that are so severe that they leave a permanent scar. The Gospel teaches that this kind of denial of pain and suffering is illusory. Even the risen and exalted Christ retains the wounds of His crucifixion. ("Jesus came and said to them, "Peace be with you." When he had said this, he showed them his hands and his side." John 20:19b-20a) Jesus Christ, who sits at the right hand of the Father, cannot fully enjoy bliss as long as anyone suffers.

The *Pneuma* of Christ that stirs within the hearts and minds of believers does not allow wounds to be healed lightly. Just as on this side of the Kingdom God's light shines in the darkness, so also the human heart sorrows over the sufferings of others and does so with the blessing of God. Indeed, the Church serves the living Christ who continues to suffer in and with the needy. (Mt 25:40)

Ruusbroec's teaching on compassion can be profitably linked with the insightful wisdom of the great 13th century Franciscan, Bonaventure. Bonaventure writes,

> In what concerns the pain of suffering, *passio,* Christ suffered more intensely in his sensibility; in what concerns the pain of co-suffering, *compassio,* he suffered more intensely in his spiritual nature. But the pain of co-suffering was greater than the pain of suffering.[53]

Passio is the pain of bodily suffering; physical, mental, and spiritual. Every human being, as a finite creature of flesh and blood, is subject to the pain of *passio*. The forms of *passio* are many. Poverty ravages millions. Chronic illness often strikes inexplicably and without warning. Accidents bring horrific injuries and even sudden death. The deleterious effects of the aging process cause debilitating hardship. Victims of violence, abuse, rape, and incest often suffer permanent scarring despite courageous determination to embrace life and to carry on as best they can. Emotional disorders and mental illnesses consume far too many souls. Depression and addiction ravage entire family units as one member's illness affects everyone—at times setting up patterns that are re-enacted from generation to generation. Broken marriages and dysfunctional family life present severe challenges to young children. Famine, pestilence, and natural disasters ravage the earth. War wreaks havoc and destruction. Yet the form of *passio* of greatest consequence is spiritual estrangement from God. Human beings possess a deep desire in the soul to see God. If this profound need goes unmet, the human spirit loses its bearings and all attempts to find true peace are thwarted.

Compassio is the pain of spiritual co-suffering. It is the pain that comes when a person joins others in their suffering, helps them to face it, and seeks to assuage it. The perfect exemplar of this form of suffering is Jesus Christ. On the cross the *compassio* He suffered was the result of taking upon Himself the estranged condition of fallen humankind. In His obedient yes to the Father, He remained faithful to the end, even to the point of undergoing (in His human nature) separation from God. This abandonment comes upon Him when the Father lays on Him the iniquity of us all. (Isaiah 53:6) "For our sake he made him to be sin who knew no sin." (II Cor 5:21a) "Christ redeemed us from the curse of the law, having become a curse for us." (Gal 3:13a)

Reflecting upon Bonaventure's analysis of the two types of suffering, *passio* and *compassio*, Hans Urs von Balthasar notes the profundity of Christ's co-suffering with estranged humanity. He argues precisely to the point when he says that it is Christ's "excess of love" that wounds His heart and makes His suffering so great:

The physical pain inflicted on Christ drew his soul into co-suffering, while the psychic pain occasioned by our sins took along the body with it, and so Christ wept over us. This spiritual suffering was the more intense, because its ultimate cause was so much deeper—offence against God and our separation from God, and also because Christ's excess of love made him the more inclined to suffer. The stronger love is, the more painful are the wounds of co-suffering.[54]

Christ's co-suffering with estranged humanity fundamentally changes the situation of the sufferer whose soul is illuminated by the light of faith. Her bodily suffering is now lightened and buoyed, and even at times completely cured, by the co-suffering of Christ. The situation of the sufferer is transformed (albeit in cruciform) because she can now cling in faith to Christ and enjoy mystical union with Him. As a consequence, she can be confident that all of her suffering is known by the Triune God. This divine embrace creates a sense of profound reassurance that God's relationship with her cannot be broken off by any future hardship—no matter how severe.

> Who will separate us from the love of Christ? Will hardship, or distress, or persecution, or famine, or nakedness, or peril, or sword?…No, in all these things we are more than conquerors through him who loved us. For I am convinced that neither death, nor life, nor angels, nor rulers, nor things present, nor things to come, nor powers, nor height, nor depth, nor anything else in all creation, will be able to separate us from the love of God in Christ Jesus our Lord. (Rom 8:35, 37-39)

No longer is a sufferer isolated and cut off from divine grace. The Son of God, the Divine Wound of Love, co-suffers with her. John Paul II writes about co-suffering:

> [In] general it can be said that almost always the individual enters suffering with a *typically human protest* and *with the*

question "why." He asks the meaning of his suffering and seeks an answer to this question on the human level. Certainly he often puts this question to God, and to Christ. Furthermore, he cannot help noticing that the One to whom he puts the question is Himself suffering and wishes to answer him from the cross, *from the heart of His own suffering.* Nevertheless, it often takes time, even a long time, for this answer to begin to be interiorly perceived. For Christ does not answer directly and He does not answer in the abstract this human questioning about the meaning of suffering. Man hears Christ's saving answer as he himself gradually becomes a sharer in the sufferings of Christ. [emphasis in text][55]

There is much wisdom in these teachings. John Paul writes that "it often takes time, even a long time" for a sufferer to hear an interior answer to her questions about suffering. The answer begins to be perceived only when the sufferer realizes that not only does Christ wish to answer her "from the cross, from the heart of His own suffering," but that she is called upon to share in His sufferings. John Paul II emphasizes the gradual nature of this answer. This answer that comes from Christ in response to the questions that the sufferer asks about the meaning of suffering does not come to her immediately or even directly. Nor does Christ answer with detailed explanations and abstract theological teachings. "Man hears Christ's saving answer as he himself gradually becomes a sharer in the sufferings of Christ."

The Apostle Paul had already experienced more than 20 years of life in Christ when he wrote in utterly profound terms of the Church's participation in the sufferings of Christ. "I want to know Christ and the power of his resurrection and the sharing of his sufferings by becoming like him in his death, if somehow I may attain the resurrection from the dead." (Phil 3:10-11) And, "But we have this treasure in earthen vessels, so that it may be made clear that this extraordinary power belongs to God and does not come from us. We are afflicted in every way, but not crushed; perplexed, but not driven to despair; persecuted, but not forsaken; struck down, but not destroyed; always carrying in the body the death of Jesus, so that the life of Jesus may also be made visible in our bodies." (II Cor 4:7-10) And again, "For as we share abundantly in Christ's sufferings, so through Christ we share abundantly in consolation too." (II Cor 1:5) But as Paul well knew, this participation in suffering is precisely that which human beings are generally determined to avoid at all costs. To illustrate this all-too-human penchant for the avoidance of suffering, it is helpful to observe the way that we tend to puzzle over Jesus' ministry of healing during His earthly life.

Healing was central to Jesus' ministry. He conducted three years of ministry, and the four Gospels give many accounts of His compassionate acts to relieve suffering. But His actions raise questions such as, why doesn't Jesus heal everyone or exorcize all those possessed by demons and why did He not raise all children who died prematurely, give sight to all of the blind, and touch and cleanse every leper? Since Jesus Christ is the all-powerful Son of God, why doesn't He just finish the job of redemption by a royal fiat? But to ask these questions is to betray the human desire to opt out of the vocation to which God has called us by virtue of creating us in His image. Although God wants us as partners, we want perfect fulfillment, we want it now, and we want God to bring it about without us. But as John Paul II has pointed out, this is not God's way. Instead, God's plan was to send His only begotten Son into the world to become incarnate as true God and true man.

In the incarnation God enters into the drama of human suffering and takes it into the life of the Trinity through Jesus' suffering and death. God in the flesh; the God who suffers! The incarnation is an embodiment of the truth that God wants us to participate in the redemptive process by becoming instruments of God's love in the world and by sharing in the sufferings of Christ for the life of the world. This sharing, this participation in the divine compassion, is a form of striving for perfect self-surrender. Practicing this compassion is another way to suffer well in union with God.

In turn, this answer that Saint John Paul II refers to in *Salvifici Doloris* gives rise to a peculiar joy that is simultaneous with ongoing suffering and hardship. It is a joy that springs from the discovery that suffering is imbued with meaning and significance when the suffering is undergone with Christ. "Now I rejoice in my sufferings for your sake, and in my flesh complete what is lacking in Christ's afflictions for the sake of his body, that is, the Church." (Col 1:24; see also James 1:2 and I Peter 4:13) This text from Colossians receives a penetrating interpretation from the 17th century Lutheran theologian Johann Gerhard:

> Just as from the personal union [of the divine and human natures of Christ] there results the sort of communication by which the Word appropriates to Himself the properties and sufferings of the assumed flesh, so also from the spiritual union of Christ and the faithful there arises the sort of communication by which Christ, through an appropriation, attributes to Himself those good and evil things that are conferred on the faithful....
>
> However, the analogy of faith and the circumstances of the text show that this refers to that mystical union that exists between the Church and Christ, and between every faithful soul and God. Because the Father and the Son make a dwelling in the hearts of the devout (John 14:23) and because Christ dwells through faith in the hearts of believers (Eph. 3:17), because the faithful are members of Christ and a mystical Body of which Christ is the Head (1 Cor. 12:12; Col. 1:18), therefore Christ appropriates to Himself the good things that are given to the devout and the evils that are inflicted on them. For this reason the apostle says explicitly, "I complete what is lacking in Christ's afflictions in my flesh for the sake of His Body, which is the Church." (Col. 1:24) And: "We carry in our body the death of Jesus Christ." (II Cor.4:10)."[56]

***

We bring this meditation to a close by observing that due to

Christ's co-suffering, the mystery of redemption takes an unexpected turn. The sufferer, having had her burden buoyed and lightened by Christ, is given the strength and fortitude that is necessary to join with Christ as she co-suffers with "the least of these." (Mat 25:40) The Christian is freed to seek ways to assuage the suffering of her neighbor even as she prays for strength to live out her life in the service of others. This is a quiet service for the good that goes largely unnoticed by the world. Gregory the Great has said it most succinctly: "In Holy Church each bears the other and is borne by him."[57]

PART TWO

Human Suffering in
Union with God

MEDITATION VI

THE WAY OF PARTICIPATION

"We should be profoundly comforted by the fact of God's being purely One without any adventitious quantity of Himself. And since this is true, I say, whatever a good man suffers for God's sake, he suffers in God, and God is with him in his suffering. If my suffering is in God and God suffers with me, how then can my suffering be painful when suffering loses its pain, and my pain is in God and my pain is God?" — Meister Eckhart

ONE THING THAT IS certain about human suffering is that suffering tends to isolate us from others. Suffering creates obstacles to intimacy with family and friends and often bars us from our wider social networks and our places of work. Suffering can scatter our sensibilities and weaken our feelings of belonging and attachment to others. Fear can seize us—causing us to lose a sense of the cohesiveness of our lives; we feel adrift, aimless. Suffering can strip us of our identity, especially if we tend to define ourselves on the basis of what we do and accomplish. In this sixth meditation we learn from Meister Eckhart how our knowledge of the Oneness of God can transform our experience of suffering.

The fact that God is One makes the subject of time and eternity central for the sufferer. How so? For the Rhineland-Flemish Mystics, and for Meister Eckhart in particular, faith is always aware of time and eternity—past, present, and future. The Gospel of Jesus Christ announces the good news that God has come so near to us in Christ that we can enjoy in the *here and now* the union with God that breaks our sense of isolation, helps us to cope with our alienation from others, calms our fears, makes firm our sense of identity as a child of God, and grants us a place in God's plan that turns aimlessness into discipleship. Eckhart instructs us to reflect on how the Oneness of God can unify our spirit as God the Father and His Son make a home in our soul. (Jn 14:23) We will learn that God does not only grant consolation to us in our suffering, but due to our union with God in Christ, our suffering contains consolation within itself because we suffer *in* God. Since this is so, Eckhart asks: What more could a sufferer want?

***

In section two of his *Book of Divine Comfort,* Meister Eckhart lists 30 conventional teachings regarding how God helps those who suffer. He makes the claim that "any one of [these teachings] should suffice to comfort the rational man in his trouble."[58] (528) In the last part of the section, Eckhart derives seven lessons from Psalm 33:19: "Many are the afflictions of the righteous, but the Lord delivers them out of them all." With each succeeding teaching his insights go deeper and deeper into the mystery of suffering. In the seventh lesson he offers what might be considered his most penetrating insight of all on this subject.

First, he cites Augustine, whom he says taught that "patience in suffering for God's sake is better, more precious, higher, and nobler than anything that a man can be deprived of against his will—which is nothing but outward goods. God knows, you will find no man who loves this world, who is so rich that he would not gladly endure great pain, and put up with it for a long time, if thereafter he might be the paramount ruler of this world." (546-547). In other words, a Christian knows that in practicing patience in suffering he can live in the sure and certain hope of eternal life in the world to come.

Second, he says, "I take it from, and in the text, that if God is with me in my suffering, what more do I want, what else do I want? Surely I want nothing else, nothing more than God if I am in a right state...Concerning this St. Bernard says, 'Lord, if thou art with us in suffering, let me suffer always, that thou mayest always be with me, so that I may always have thee.'" (547) Note his oft-used phrase, "if I am in a right state." This is an example of the high bar that Eckhart sets for Christian discipleship. He seems to come close to suggesting that Christians are out of bounds if they pray to God for an end to their own suffering or that of their loved ones. Is he selling short the healing that comes to those who are long-suffering in prayer? Does he think that Paul was wrong to ask the Lord three times to remove the thorn in his flesh? (II Cor 12:8) And what are we to make of Mat 7:7, when Jesus assures His followers saying, "Ask, and it will be given to you." Eckhart's is a severe teaching and one that echoes that of St. Bernard. But he emphasizes that his instructions hold "for the good and perfected people, who have so absorbed and assimilated the essence of all virtues that these virtues emanate from them naturally, without their seeking; and above all there must dwell in them the worthy life and lofty teachings of our Lord Jesus Christ."[59] He is directing these comments to those who have placed their desire for union with God without intermediary above any concerns that they may have for their own personal suffering. He is speaking to them in hyperbolic speech in order to drive home the great blessing that comes to those who are graced with God's presence: "[If] God is with me in my suffering, what more do I want, what else do I want?"

Third, "I say that God's being with us in suffering means that He suffers with me Himself. Truly, he who knows the truth knows that I speak the truth. God suffers with man, indeed, He suffers in His fashion before, and far more than that man suffers for His sake. So I declare, if God Himself wills to suffer, then it is only right that I should suffer, for if it is well with me, then I want what God wants. I pray everyday..."Lord, thy will be done," and yet, when God wants suffering, I complain...which is quite wrong." (547)

Curiously, these teachings fail to use Trinitarian language. Does

Eckhart adequately enflesh the Christian God who became incarnate in Jesus Christ? After all He entered bodily into the world, suffered, died, was buried, and was raised from the dead. Contrast Eckhart's approach with John Paul II's, who comments upon this text from Matthew 26, "Then he said to [Peter, and the two sons of Zebedee]: "My soul is very sorrowful, even to death; remain here, and watch with me." And going a little farther he fell on his face and prayed, "My Father, if it be possible, let this cup pass from me; nevertheless, not as I will, but as thou wilt.":

> [These words] prove the truth of that love which the only-begotten Son gives to the Father in His obedience. At the same time, they attest to the truth of His suffering. The words of that prayer of Christ in Gethsemane *prove the truth of love through the truth of suffering.* Christ's words confirm with all simplicity this human truth of suffering to its very depths: suffering is the undergoing of evil before which man shudders. He says: Let it pass from me," just as Christ says in Gethsemane. His words also attest to this unique and incomparable depth and intensity of suffering which only the man who is the only-begotten Son could experience; they attest to that *depth and intensity* which the prophetic words quoted above in their own way help us to understand. Not of course completely (for this we would have to penetrate the divine-human mystery of the subject), but at least they help us to understand that difference (and at the same time the similarity) which exists between every possible form of human suffering and the suffering of the God-man. Gethsemane is the place where precisely this suffering, in all the truth expressed by the prophet concerning evil experienced in it, *is revealed as it were definitively before the eyes of Christ's soul.*[60] [emphasis in text]

John Paul II suggests that Jesus' yes to the Father is the quintessential model for a Christian's believing response to suffering. Unlike Eckhart, the Pope holds that evil and suffering understandably prompt the heartfelt prayer: "Let this pass from me." But he also calls for an acceptance of suffering if it be God's will. And this acceptance will be a willing participation in Jesus' yes to the Father ("Thy will be done") in the power of the Spirit. John Paul II's concern is a pastoral one, so he allows for human weakness and sin. Eckhart's severe approach tries to take with ultimate seriousness the sufficiency of God's grace.

Eckhart continues his third lesson: "I also declare of a surety that God is so fond of suffering with us and for us if *we* suffer purely for God's sake, that He suffers without suffering. To suffer is such joy to Him that suffering for Him is no suffering. And so, if we were in a right state, our suffering would be no suffering but a joy and a comfort." [emphasis in text] (547) If it be asked how it is that he "suffers without suffering," it may be recalled that Eckhart's teaching is always traversing that vague boundary line that lies between ordinary human existence and the mystical state of consciousness in which the human spirit detaches itself from the five senses and the images created in the mind. When he says, "He suffers without suffering," he is witnessing to the strange blessing that comes from union with God.

Fourth, "I say that a friend's sympathy naturally eases my pain. So, if the suffering a human being shares with me brings comfort, how much more will God's sympathy [*mitleiden*] comfort me!" (548) Bernard McGinn comments on this statement, noting that here there is a "play on the two meanings of *mitleiden*: 'suffering with another' and 'sympathy.' In fact the German word is a literal rendering of the Latin *compassio* (Greek sympatheia)."[61] (Meditation V was a reflection upon the meaning of this *compassio*.)

Fifth, "[If] I were ready and willing to suffer with a human being I was fond of and who was fond of me, then it is right that I should be willing to suffer with God, who suffers with me for the love He bears me." (548) Eckhart argues that because human beings are often willing to suffer for other human beings, they ought to respond all the more to the call to suffer with God who has loved them first and has suffered with them out of that love. Paul could say, "I have been crucified with Christ; it is no longer I who live, but Christ who lives in me." Eckhart also states that "since God suffers with me for the love He bears me" so also will I gladly suffer with God and in God. He restates this same idea in even clearer terms in lesson six.

Sixth, "I declare if God suffers in advance, before I suffer, and if I suffer for God's sake, then indeed all my suffering, however great and manifold it may be, can easily turn to comfort and joy. It is a natural truth that if a man does something [but he does it] for another purpose, then that for which he does it is closer to his heart, and what he does is further from his heart and does not concern him except for the sake of that on account of which and for which it was done… So…when a man does everything for God's sake, that God is the mediator and closest to the soul, and then nothing can touch a man's heart and soul without perforce losing its bitterness through God and God's sweetness, becoming pure sweetness before ever it can touch the man's heart…" (548)

Like so many other statements by Eckhart, the denseness of this teaching begs for a concrete illustration from everyday life, so I will offer one. In war a Marine on the battlefield is not so much motivated by patriotism for his country or even for the desire to win. Rather, the Marine wishes to prove himself to his comrades and to do right by them. If he suffers a dreadful wound in battle, the Marine considers this the price that he must be prepared to pay if he is to keep faith with his buddies. The suffering is not the focus; the focus is on *semper fidelis*, always being faithful. In the same way, a believer seeks above all to prove himself faithful to God for the love that God has first shown to him.

Eckhart concludes lesson six: "Now we can clearly perceive how well, and in how various ways, a good man is consoled on all sides in suffering, in sorrow, and in action. One way, if he suffers and works for God's sake, and another way, if he is in divine love. And a man can also tell and know if he is doing all his works for God's sake, and if he is in God's love; for assuredly, if a man finds himself woeful and disconsolate, to that extent his work was not done for God alone." (548-549)

In his seventh and final lesson, Meister Eckhart presents one of his most helpful insights into how the God and Father of Jesus Christ relates to human suffering by highlighting the importance of the *Oneness* of God:

> The seventh point about saying that God is with us in suffering and suffers with us is, we should be profoundly comforted by the fact of God's being purely One without any adventitious quantity of Himself. And since this is true, I say, whatever a good man suffers for God's sake, he suffers in God, and God is with him in his suffering. If my suffering is in God and God suffers with me, how then can my suffering be painful when suffering loses its pain, and my pain is in God and my pain *is* God? In truth, as God is truth and wherever I find truth I find God, the truth—so likewise, neither more nor less, whenever I find pure suffering in God and for God, there I find God, my suffering. (549) [emphasis in text]

How shall we understand Eckhart's statement: "How then can my suffering be painful when suffering loses its pain, and my pain is in God and my pain *is* God?" God is pure activity, so there can be no suffering in God as God. Yet Eckhart dares to say, "my pain *is* God." The statement only makes orthodox sense when it is connected, as it is here, with God's Oneness. Donald F. Duclow has done some good work on this question. He writes,

> [For Eckhart] God is not only our fellow sufferer but our very suffering somehow becomes divine. This paradox places Eckhart's art of suffering and consolation squarely within his metaphysics and mystical theology; for Eckhart frames this declaration in terms of divine unity…Divine unity is among Eckhart's most pervasive themes. In the tradition of Neoplatonism he conceives divine unity as prior to all distinction and opposition, and as enfolding all multiplicity in its simplicity. In virtue of this ontological priority "God is one in Himself and separated from everything else," radically other than finite,

distinct beings; yet this very difference simultaneously renders the one God "indistinct" from all things, because all opposites so coincide in divine unity that "everything that is in God is God Himself."[62]

Duclow's reading of Eckhart penetrates to the nub of one of Eckhart's chief insights. For Eckhart it is not enough to say that God brings consolation to combat suffering. Insofar as suffering is centered upon God "suffering *bears consolation within itself*."[63] In faith "my pain is God" because God is purely One. For Eckhart this union is nothing less than a proleptic anticipation of the beatific vision in a mystical *eternal now*. Mystical union with God reflects the truth of these words of Christ: "Truly, truly, I say to you, the hour is coming, *and now is*, when the dead will hear the voice of the Son of God, and those who hear will live." (Jn 5:25) There is a sense in which the Kingdom of God comes in its fullness in the here and now; an eternal now. Thus Eckhart can state,

> All the goodness of outward suffering comes forth and flows from the will, as I have written before. And therefore, whatever a good man would suffer, and is ready and eager to suffer for God's sake, that he does suffer before God's face, for God's sake in God. (550)

Since God is One, the person of faith suffers "before God's face, for God's sake in God." It follows that the Oneness of God means that union with God is not only a possibility, it is a reality for every believer who, in cooperation with the work of the Spirit, directs his will toward one goal: striving for perfect self-surrender. A believer's *prayerful participation* in the Oneness of God in the eternal now is another way to suffer well in union with God.

But if this is so, why has this aspect of suffering received so little notice in the Church? Surely it is due to human weakness. Eckhart asks: What more could sufferers want than to suffer in God? But alas, most of us, if we are honest, would respond to that question by saying, "I want suffering abolished." But Eckhart's reply to that demand is as clear as it is Christ centered:

> St. Paul says that God chastens all whom He accepts and receives as sons (cf. Heb. 12:6). Sonship involves suffering. Because God's Son could not suffer in the Godhead and in eternity, the heavenly Father sent him into time, to become man and suffer. So, if you want to be God's son and yet do not want to suffer, you are wrong. (545-546)

The believer's adoption as a child of God does not eliminate suffering. But Eckhart celebrates the Oneness of God. He reasons, God is One; therefore, whatever a good person suffers he suffers in God. Therefore his pain is in God—and since there is no distinction in God—his pain *is* God. But this means that when he is ready and eager to suffer for God's sake, he suffers before God's face, in God. But to say this is to say that he suffers in mystical union with God beyond all distinction and without intermediary!

MEDITATION VII

THE WAY OF LOVE

When the soul awakens to its true vocation, the stubborn hu-
man demand for a theodicy—a justification of God in the face
of suffering—is redirected by grace into the sphere of the sublime
love of God. So, rise out of the ensnaring foulness of temporal de-
lights. Open the eyes of your mind and see what you are, where
you are, and where you are going; and then at once you will
have the strength to grasp the reason of all these things.

"DEWEY, LOOK AT THE world. Look at it!" This was the response
of a friend recently when I told her that I was working on a
book having to do with God and human suffering. I have known her
for many years and I have come to appreciate her thoughtful point
of view. She is a young woman who has a great love and appreciation
for nature, wildlife, and human life. She loves the world. She wants
to do what is right. But she is profoundly troubled by the state of the
world. She does not believe in God. Her emphatic reply to me con-
tained at least part of the reason for her disbelief. She seemed to be
saying, "If your God of love exists, why is God's creation so messed
up?" This "why" question begs for a theodicy, for a defense of God.

The philosopher Leibniz coined the term *theodicy* (God-justice) to
denote any attempt to vindicate divine providence in the face of evil
and suffering. In this meditation Henry Suso takes the position that

a rational theodicy that seeks to marshal arguments within the limits of reason alone in defense of God's goodness cannot succeed because we humans (as mere creatures) cannot justify the Creator. But Suso would say to my friend, "Yes, look at the world. It is true that there is every reason to despair at the depths to which the world has fallen. But God has set the process of redemption in motion by revealing to that needy world a divine love that seeks to reclaim the world, renewing it in Christ. Open your heart to this love. Do not allow the fallen world to keep you from that love." But Suso does allow that even people of faith will raise questions about the mystery of evil and suffering; they will ask questions, seeking understanding. Meditation VII will show that while Suso acknowledges the persistence of the "why" question, the only answer that can be hoped for in this life is the soul's recognition of the sublime love of God.

***

Having completed six meditations it may be surprising to some that the subject of bodily suffering has not received more attention than it has so far in this study. There are many texts in which our mystics speak explicitly about bodily suffering in relation to the second stage of the mystical life—the middle stage that follows the initial jubilation yet precedes the achievement of union with God. Suso can be especially graphic regarding the torments that his body underwent in the course of his life. And Tauler speaks of the strange bodily illnesses (which we might label psychosomatic today) that afflicted devoted disciples of his day. In this way Tauler helped his flock to better understand their own physical ailments and to see them as signs of progress along the mystical pathway to God. The reason I have not highlighted these discussions is the fact that the distinctive contribution that the five mystics made regarding the subject of God and human suffering grew out of their ardent focus on union with God without intermediary. It is interesting to point out that while these mystics were *not* guilty of avoiding the subject of bodily suffering, Alasdair MacIntyre has observed that many intellectuals in the

Western tradition *have* been guilty of avoiding the reality of suffering in their work:

> [In the] history of Western moral philosophy…from Plato to Moore and since there are usually, with some rare exceptions, only passing references to human vulnerability and affliction and to the connections between them and our dependence on others…And when the ill, the injured and the otherwise disabled are presented in the pages of moral philosophy books, it is almost always exclusively as possible subjects of benevolence by moral agents who are themselves presented as though they were continuously rational, healthy and untroubled.[64]

In our day, as in every age, it is common for people to try to find ways to distance themselves from a direct confrontation with suffering. One such distancing strategy is to turn the subject of God and suffering into an *intellectual* problem. The problem is established by asking the classic question of theodicy: If God is both good and all-powerful, why does God allow the suffering of innocents? Or David Hume's well-known formulation may be approvingly cited: "Is [God] willing to prevent evil, but not able? Then he is impotent. Is he able, but not willing? Then he is malevolent. Is he both able and willing? Whence then is evil?"[65]

Henry Suso was critical of this kind of an approach to suffering. To be sure, he readily concedes that it is true that faith's shadow, doubt, does at times prompt believers to ask these very questions. But he taught that believers dare not shrink before such doubt because faith insists that the question of God and human suffering is framed by *the new reality of love* that has been disclosed in Christ. The format of Henry Suso's *Wisdom's Watch Upon the Hours* is a series of conversations between a disciple and Divine Wisdom. At the beginning of one important exchange, Wisdom places suffering firmly within the context of this new reality of love when he says, "As the Father has loved me, I also love mine. The disciple is not above his master." (Jn 15:9) This declaration by Wisdom provides the context within which the following dialogue proceeds:

> Disciple: Now, if it is permitted to speak, I know what I want to say. See, this is what I am lamenting, this is what I bewail, why I am groaning and sighing from the bottom of my heart. Hear, I beg, your servant. Look at those who are saying: "There is no salvation for him in his God. They labor in vain who serve God." And why? They say that their reason is...the constant tribulation of the just. Nevertheless they will add that this is why you have so few friends, because you are accustomed to play this kind of game with them...(153-154)[66]

The disciple reports that one reason God seems to have so few friends is that the just are permitted to suffer. The disciple is not himself questioning God's goodness. He asks God why He does not go about His redemptive activity in such a way so as to spare the innocent from suffering and death because in so doing God would gain more followers. Wisdom at first responds by pointing out that God's ways are beyond human knowing:

> Wisdom: This question of theirs often perturbs minds that possess little faith or knowledge ...they do not know how incomprehensible are God's judgments, and the depth of the riches of his wisdom and his knowledge, and that God does not see as man sees. For man looks only at present things, but God at what is to come and is everlasting. But you, who have been brought up differently in our spiritual philosophy, stand up, and with your mind pass above everything that can be seen; "for the things that are seen are temporal, but the things that are not seen are eternal." [II Cor 4:18] (154-155)

Wisdom next urges Christians to remember their nature and destiny. The following exhortation is packed with insights that draw the mind deep into thoughtful reflection:

So rise out of the ensnaring foulness of temporal delights. Open the eyes of your mind, and see what you are, where you are, and where you are going; and then at once you will have the strength to grasp the reason of all these things. For you are a mirror of the godhead, because God can be reflected in you more clearly than in other created things; you are an image of the Trinity, because his image can shine back in you; you are a pattern of eternity, because you can rejoice in an inviolable incorruption. And just as I am in my essence infinite, so the desire of your soul is like a boundless abyss to fill—which not all the joys together of the world could suffice, no more than a single drop could fill the vastness of an ocean. (155)

Marvelous! Suso teaches that a person who is suffering must open her mind to recall her origin in God, live in the now in union with God, and foresee her fulfillment in God. He also says that if she fails to acknowledge her rightful abode in God, she will blame God for her suffering. Wisdom Personified suggests that if a believer persists in questioning divine providence in the face of suffering by insisting upon a theodicy, it is an indication that she has forgotten four vital things. First, she has forgotten her nature as a "mirror of the godhead." Second, she has forgotten her identity as one who is "an image of the Trinity." Third, she has forgotten her calling, as God's child, to reflect "a pattern of divine eternity." Fourth, she has forgotten to acknowledge that the "boundless abyss" of the deepest desire of her soul will be fulfilled because she is being drawn by Christ's infinite essence to a fullness of joy in the life to come.

As mentioned earlier it is important to keep in mind that all of this was prefaced by the words, "As the Father has loved me, I also love mine. The disciple is not above his master." (Jn 15:9) The conclusion is clear. When the soul reawakens to its true vocation, the intellectual demand for a satisfying rational theodicy is redirected by grace into the sphere of God's love. Perfect self-surrender to this love is another way to suffer well in union with God.

John Paul II concurs:

But in order to perceive the true answer to the "why" of suffering, we must look to the revelation of divine love, the ultimate source of the meaning of everything that exists. Love is also the richest source of the meaning of suffering which always remains a mystery: we are conscious of the insufficiency and inadequacy of our explanations. Christ causes us to enter into the mystery and to discover the 'why' of suffering, as far as we are capable of grasping the sublimity of divine love.[67]

John Paul II stresses that the questions that arise about suffering cannot be answered by mere logic and argumentation. Instead a rational theodicy must give way to the discovery of the why of suffering that comes when the sufferer begins to participate in divine love.

Similarly, on April 27, 2014, Pope Francis spoke of how only the suffering love of God can enable us to overcome our rational doubts about the existence of a merciful God. He did so at the mass and canonization ceremony for Pope John XXIII and Pope John Paul II. His homily draws upon the text (John 20:24-28) in which Thomas insists that "unless I see in his hands the print of the nails, and place my finger in the mark of the nails, and place my hand in his side, I will not believe." Christ then appears to him, and showing him his wounds says, "Peace be with you." Pope Francis remarks on this exchange:

> The wounds of [the risen] Jesus are a scandal, a stumbling block for faith. Yet they are also the test of faith. That's why on the body of the risen Christ the wounds never pass away. They remain. For those wounds are the enduring sign of God's love for us. They're essential for believing in God. Not for believing that God exists, but for believing that God is love, mercy and faithfulness.

The spiritual path that sufferers take that can slowly lead them to understand the "why" of suffering often begins with mortifying shame. This shame indicates that their relationship with God is broken. Contrition and the desire to be baptized in the name of the Triune God is an open acknowledgement of estrangement from God. The convert is responding to the love of God that has been "poured into his heart through the Holy Spirit." (Rom 5:5b) The life-giving *Pneuma* of Christ performs His redemptive work in the ground of the sinner's soul. Seeing him from a distance, the Father has compassion on him, and, so to speak, runs out to embrace and welcome His prodigal child home. (Lk 15:20) This love that the Son shares with the Father is the Spirit of adoption through which believers become children of God. (Rom 8:15)

Initiates are led to deny themselves by imitating the self-humbling love of Christ. They allow Christ to revivify their hearts. The initiate at baptism is taken-up into the *koinonia* (intimate sharing) of the three Persons of the Trinity. The Father declares, "You are my beloved Son, in whom I am well pleased." God's kindness leads the initiate to this repentance. (Rom 2:4) By the workings of divine grace, the initiate is moved by love to surrender his creaturely will-to-control back to the Creator. The decision is aided by the grace of God, but is made freely. To be named a child of God fills the heart of the convert with a desire to praise God, but the words to do so feel painfully inadequate. Even here there is suffering. Suso hints at the subtle but very real suffering that he experiences due to the frustration that he feels at not being able to adequately praise God:

> But what shall I say? I know myself, Lord, to be unworthy to praise you, yet nonetheless I pray at least that other created beings, splendid in their nobility, may deign to make up what is wanting in my imperfect being. So I ask, and this comes from the desire of my whole heart, that the planets in their courses and the starry heaven, radiant with its most pellucid light, and, too, the flowering plants, lovely in their vernal beauty and adorned with their fair hues, and the burning desires of love in the hearts of all who yearn for you with a most fervent longing, may praise you and bless you for ever and ever. My heart melts, my Lord, only to recall your praise,

my senses are dazed, my reason is astonished, my words falter, and turned inward upon myself, I sigh more deeply. For I find in myself some desire, for which I have not words and which transcends every natural faculty, to praise you, the highest good, and yet I mourn that this is not possible, and that I must leave it unspoken. For if I wish to compare you with intelligent or intellectual created things, I find beyond doubt that you infinitely surpass everything that has been created. If I consider what is good, what is sweet, what is lovely or gracious, I know for very truth that you are more, beyond all telling, in grace than are all these, and, what is far more, that you are the spirit and the essence of them all. (293-294)

***

To the blessings of Holy Baptism, the Lord adds those of the Sacrament of the Eucharist. Holy Communion is the climax of every Mass. What is this gift that the Church receives in the Eucharist, a gift which is finally all but impossible to put into words? In Suso's book a devout Christian disciple asks divine Wisdom Personified, "What will you give by your presence to a man receiving you devoutly in the sacrament?" Wisdom replies, "And I ask, from where does this question come? Are you a lover, or are you a hired servant...Is it love you are seeking, or the reward of love? What have I to give that is better, that is more profitable, or that is more precious than myself?" (281) Suso sounds a major theme of the theology of the Rhineland Mystics, which we will formulate thus: God's gracious indwelling in the ground of the soul has an element of ultimate sufficiency; it *is* salvation. So it is enough for the sufferer to know that the Giver is the Gift. In the Eucharist the real presence of Christ in the Supper is a means of grace through which God's love rules in the human heart.

This presence of Christ in the Eucharist carries with it a profound union of Christ with the Church gathered. "The bread that we break, is it not a communion in the body of Christ? Because there is one bread, we who are many are one body, for we all partake of the one bread." (I Cor 10:16b-17). John Chrysostom interprets this text in this way: "The bread that we break, is it not communion [koinonia] with the body of Christ? Why not say *participation* (metoche)? Because he [Paul] has wanted to say something more and to indicate the greatness of the union. In fact we communicate not principally (monon) when we partake and eat but when we are united."[68] [emphasis in text] Speaking of communion and participation, John D. Zizioulas writes:

At first sight these terms seem to be interchangeable in the Greek Fathers; however a clear distinction was deliberately and significantly made in their use: participation is used only for creatures in their relation with God, and never for God in his relation to creation...[Thus] the truth of creation is a *dependent* truth, while the truth of God's being is *communion* in itself...[And] this conclusion implies that reality or the truth of created existence cannot affirm itself by itself. *God and the world cannot be ontologically placed side by side as self-defined entities.* Creaturely truth is dependent upon something else, in which it participates; this is truth as *communion by participation* (as compared with God, who is truth as *communion without participation*). Thus we cannot say that creation is truth according to its own "nature." Once more, the idea of truth leads us ultimately not to the "nature" of things, as with the Greeks, but to life and communion of beings.[69] [emphasis in text]

Zizioulas' assertion that "creaturely truth is dependent upon something else, in which it participates; this is truth as communion by participation" is in basic agreement with the spirit of Rhineland-Flemish mysticism. The Rhineland-Flemish Mystics agree that a human being has no real existence apart from God; God must breathe life-giving Spirit into her. In the Eucharist—the most vivid illustration of communion by participation—communicants, by means of this union, participate in the Christian Mystery. Those who live out of this Mystery undergo a spiritual journey, a joyous passage from death to life, through the cross to the resurrection which was once and for all accomplished by Christ. The Mystery is re-presented by the Church in the celebration of the Mass for the life of the world. On this side of the Kingdom, it is in partaking of the Eucharist that sufferers are most intimately united with God. In Holy Communion the community of sufferers receives the consolation of the Comforter. This succor comes even to those who are so weighed down that the best they can do is bow their heads and breathe forth their sorrow. Edgar Lee Masters wrote about this Communion:

Aaron Hatfield[70]

Better than granite, Spoon River,
Is the memory-picture you keep of me
Standing before the pioneer men and women
There at Concord Church on Communion day,
Speaking in broken voice of the peasant youth
Of Galilee who went to the city
And was killed by bankers and lawyers;
My voice mingling with the June wind
That blew over wheat fields from Atterbury,
While the white stones in the burying ground
Around the Church simmered in the summer sun.
And there, though my own memories
Were too great to bear, were you, O pioneers,
With bowed heads breathing forth your sorrow
For the sons killed in battle and the daughters
And the little children who vanished in life's morning,
Or at the intolerable hour of noon.
But in those moments of tragic silence,
When the wine and bread were passed,
Came the reconciliation for us—
Us the ploughmen and the hewers of wood,
Us the peasants, brothers of the peasant of Galilee—
To us came the Comforter
And the consolation of tongues of flame!

***

Yet, it must be said that there is a sobering counterpoint to this theme of communion: Believers must come to accept that one of the fruits of suffering well for Christ is becoming repugnant to the world. This acceptance typically comes slowly for the sufferer because of how painful it is for her to face this truth. But if and when the believer comes to this acceptance, God leads her to discover yet another precious dimension of discipleship: the sufferer learns that her suffering can be a strange kind of blessing because suffering conforms her more closely to the image of Christ. In the following excerpt, eternal Wisdom leads the servant to the realization that under God's guidance believers can come to see their suffering as a vehicle of divine grace. In the course of this dialogue, simplistic platitudes and easy answers are dispensed with as Wisdom Personified guides the servant of faith ever deeper into the mysteries of suffering.[71]

Response of *eternal Wisdom*: Now, listen to the music from the taut strings of a person suffering for God (and see) how rich it sounds and how sweet the tones are: In the eyes of the world suffering is repugnant, but in my sight it is something immeasurably valuable. Suffering quenches my anger and wins my favor. Suffering makes a person worthy of my love because a person in suffering resembles me. Suffering is a hidden good that no one can buy. If someone knelt before me for a hundred years asking to suffer well, he would not deserve it. It turns an earthly man into a heavenly man. Suffering estranges one from the world, but it affords constant intimacy with me. It decreases (the number of one's) friends, but it increases grace. If I am to become someone's friend, he must be completely rejected and forsaken by the whole world. This is the safest and shortest path, and the most perfect. Look, the person who really knows how advantageous suffering is should accept it from God as a valuable gift....

And a little later, *eternal Wisdom* continues:

Patience in suffering is a living sacrifice. It is a sweet fragrance of precious balsam before my divine countenance. It is a marvel springing up in front of the whole heavenly army. Never was there as great astonishment at a knight performing well in a tournament as the astonishment of the whole heavenly host at a person suffering well. All the saints are the cupbearers of a person suffering because they have tasted it already and call out with one voice that it is free of any poison and is a health-bringing potion. Patience in suffering is greater than raising the dead or performing other marvelous signs. It is the narrow path that gloriously reaches the gates of heaven. Suffering makes one equal to the martyrs… In eternity it leads the singing of a new dance song with a sweet voice and free spirit, a song that the angelic hosts could never sing because they never experienced suffering. Put briefly: In the world those who suffer are called poor, but by me they are called the blessed because they are my elect.

This word from eternal Wisdom brings a joyous response from the servant and prompts the following exchange:

The *servant*: Truly, it becomes very apparent that you are eternal Wisdom because you know how to bring truth out into the open so vividly that no one is able to have the slightest doubt about it. No wonder the person for whom you make suffering such a joy can endure suffering. Lord, by your sweet words you have brought about not just that I shall find all suffering much more bearable and shall endure it in joy, my Lord and devoted Father; but also, I kneel before you today and praise you earnestly for my present suffering and for severe past suffering as well, which seemed so immense to me because it appeared so menacing.

Eternal Wisdom: What, then, is your opinion now?

The *servant*: Lord, this is what I really think: When with loving eyes I look at you, a joy for my heart to gaze upon, all the severe sufferings, with which you, like a father, have tried me, and at the sight of which your saintly friends shuddered, were like the sweet dew of springtime.

MEDITATION VIII

THE WAY OF ACCEPTANCE

The soul must embrace all suffering—deserved or undeserved—as coming from the hand of God. Welcome, bitter affliction, full of grace! But be of good cheer. The Lord is not far away. Cling to the rock of the true and living faith. Your anguish will soon be over, though in this state your soul cannot conceive that this insufferable darkness could ever give way to light. Then, at last, God comes and raises the soul to the highest stage, giving the believer new eyes to see—leading him out of himself and into Him.

LITTLE CHILDREN SING, "JESUS loves me this I know, for the Bible tells me so." This expresses a simple truth. But as our faith matures, we are called to deepen our understanding of God's love. Mysteriously, there is a *horrific* dimension to divine love. Those who mocked Christ at the crucifixion taunted Him, wondering why God was not intervening for Him if He was the Messiah. Why indeed! As Jesus suffers abandonment on the cross, His God and Father is silent; seemingly absent. In this meditation we learn again that a servant is not above his master. Just as Christ, in His human nature, suffered desolation on the cross, so also will His disciples undergo desolation of body, mind, and spirit. Johannes Tauler shows us the heart of a pastor when he counsels us to embrace all of the suffering that comes to us: "Welcome bitter affliction, full of grace!" In the following text, John Paul II shows us how to enter into the mystery of what Tauler calls the desolation stage of Christian discipleship:

> When Christ says: "My God, my God, why have you abandoned me?", His words are not only an expression of that abandonment which many times found expression in the Old Testament, especially in the psalms and in particular in that Psalm 22 from which come the words quoted. One can say that *these words on abandonment are born at the level of that inseparable union of the Son with the Father, and are born because the Father "laid on him the iniquity of us all."* [emphasis added][72]

In His suffering and death, Christ takes upon Himself the full weight of human sin. God's Son suffers in the place of fallen humanity who has turned away from God's covenant promises by refusing to be bound by the limitations imposed by good and evil, morality, and the will of God. In a felicitous phrase John Paul II says that out of the darkness of the abandonment that is "born at the level of that inseparable union of the Son with the Father" came the redemption of humankind. "While we were yet sinners Christ died for the ungodly." (Rom 5:6) The disciples of Jesus must travel down a similar road that leads from cross to resurrection.

***

In a sermon on I Peter 3:8 ("Beloved, be you all of one mind in prayer"), Tauler outlines what he sees as the three stages of the spiritual life: jubilation, desolation, and divinization.[73] The greatest suffering is in the desolation stage. The lesson to be learned from this sermon is that suffering must always be viewed within the context of the believer's journey of faith; suffering is always suffering *on the way to God*. Tauler begins his sermon by sounding three themes: The inner life of the Trinity, the nobility of the human creature who has been made in the image of that Trinity, and the faculties of the soul in human beings that prompt them to desire life in God.

First, there is Tauler's description of the inner life of the Triune God:

> The heavenly Father, in His divine attribute of Fatherhood, is pure activity. Everything in Him is activity, for it is by the act of self-comprehension that He begets His beloved Son, and both in an ineffable embrace breathe forth the Holy Spirit. Their mutual love is an eternal, essential activity of the Persons, and yet they rest in themselves in the uncreated being and simplicity of the divine Essence. And here there is a silent, simple enjoying, a simple consuming of God's being, and activity and enjoyment are one. (138)

The active life of the holy Trinity is an eternal begetting of the Son by the Father. Out of their mutual love, they rest in themselves and breathe forth the Holy Spirit. This same activity and rest take place in the ground of the human soul when God revivifies the soul. In this justifying act of God, the focus is on both essential activity and eternal rest as dual aspects of God's essential being. This alternation between activity and rest will be central to the spiritual life of every person who is redeemed by Christ's saving activity.

Second, there is Tauler's description of the nobility of God's creation:

> Now since God has made His creatures in His likeness, activity is inherent in all of them. The firmament, the sun and stars, and far above them Angels and men—all are active in their proper way. There is no flower so small, no blade of grass so tiny, that the heavenly bodies did not work in them. And, above all, God Himself is at work in them. Is it surprising, then, that man, that noble creature, fashioned in God's Image, should resemble Him in His activity? Since he is endowed with faculties in God's Image, ought he not be like Him in

being? This noble creature must act with far greater nobility than created things, such as the heavens, which are devoid of reason. The whole of creation should follow man because of his likeness to God both in action and in contemplation. No matter in what direction man turns with his higher and lower faculties, he is forever active; and each of his faculties acts in a way commensurate to its object. Be it God or some created thing, man's faculties act upon an object according to its nature. (138-139)

Tauler argues that because human beings are made in the image of God, they ought to resemble God in being and in activity. God in Christ seeks to bring this resemblance about.

Third, he describes how the soul of Jesus Christ embodies this nobility:

Now, whoever makes God and heavenly things the object of his activity, leaving temporal concerns far behind, his works would indeed become divinized. The noble, dearest soul of Our Lord Jesus Christ was in its highest faculties unceasingly turned toward the Godhead; from His first day on earth. His soul was directed toward that goal. His soul then possessed the same beatific knowledge of the Father as He does now. In the lower faculties He was active, moving and suffering, for, in Our Lord's earthly life, joy, work, and sorrow were joined. Even when He hung dying upon the Cross, He possessed in His highest faculties the same joy in God's presence as He does now in Heaven. And all those of us who would faithfully follow Him in our surrender to what is divine, in whom activity and joyful contemplation have become one, they will resemble Him closest after death, when their whole being will be rapt in essential and eternal joy. (139)

How should these claims regarding the inner life of Jesus be understood? The claims flow from Tauler's philosophical and theological presuppositions, and are inferences he makes based on the divinity of Christ. Together with Eckhart he reasons that because Jesus is both true God and true man, as the Son of God, His relationship with the Father is inviolable. It is interesting to note that Wolfhart Pannenberg agrees with Tauler that Jesus suffered and died "according to his human nature." But he is not satisfied to leave it at that, so he argues that there is also a sense in which the Son of God suffered "in the person of the eternal Son."

> The passion of Jesus Christ is not an event which concerned only the human nature that the divine Logos assumed, as though it did not affect in any way the eternal placidity of the Trinitarian life of God. In the death of Jesus the deity of his God and Father was at issue…To be dogmatically correct, indeed, we have to say that the Son of God, though he suffered and died himself, did so according to his human nature. Even to speak directly of the death of God in the Son is a reverse Monophysitism. Nevertheless, we have to say that Jesus was affected by suffering and death on the cross in person, i.e., in the person of the eternal Son. In his extreme humiliation, in his acceptance of death, Jesus took upon himself the ultimate consequence of his self-distinction from the Father and precisely in so doing showed himself to be the Son of the Father. Nor can the Father be thought of as unaffected by the passion of his Son if it is true that God is love. The cross throws doubt not merely on the divine power of Jesus but also on the deity of the Father as Jesus proclaimed him. To this extent we may speak of the Father's sharing of the suffering of the Son, his sympathy with the passion.[74]

Perhaps with this line of argument, Pannenberg, a Lutheran, is drawing from *The Book of Concord* which—building upon Chalcedon's definition—argued that the suffering of the Son entails a *communicatio idiomatum* (communion of the characteristics) between Christ's human nature and His divine nature. The *Solid Declaration,*

Article viii, states,

> Because of this personal union, without which this kind of
> true communion of the natures is unthinkable and impossible,
> not only the bare human nature (which possesses the char-
> acteristics of suffering and dying) suffered for the sins of the
> entire world, but the Son of God himself suffered (according
> to the assumed human nature) and, according to our simple
> Christian creed, truly died—although the divine nature can
> neither suffer nor die.[75]

In contrast to Pannenberg's position, Tauler held that the earthly
Jesus enjoyed the beatific vision within His soul in His higher faculties even while in His lower faculties He experienced joy, work, and
sorrow. A contemporary theologian sheds light on this question in
his book, *The Suffering of the Impassible God, The Dialectics of Patristic
Thought.* In it Paul Gavrilyuk revisits the heated debates within the
Church during the first four centuries of the Christian era that cul-
minated in the orthodox insistence that God the Father is impassible
(does not suffer) and God the Son suffered according to His human
nature. I quote at length from his conclusion:

> After a prolonged struggle, the conciliar mind of the church
> came to the uncompromising recognition that in Christ it was
> God the Creator who entered into his creation to redeem it,
> and that the logic of our salvation required Christ's undimin-
> ished divinity. This newly achieved precision sharpened the
> tension between Christ's divine identity, marked by impassi-
> bility, and his human experiences to a degree never encoun-
> tered before. It was inevitable that the question, how precisely
> was God involved in the human suffering of Christ? would be
> raised with a new force.
> [It is in this historical context that] Cyril of Alexandria rec-
> ognized that the predication of suffering to the divine nature
> alone would render the assumption of humanity superfluous,

whereas the opposite extreme, the attribution of suffering to the human nature alone would jeopardize divine involvement...[So it was crucial] to differentiate between that which the Word undergoes in his own nature and the experiences that can only be attributed to the Word by virtue of his appropriation of the human nature.

It was precisely this differentiation that Cyril of Alexandria was concerned to sustain [so] Cyril made the self-emptying of the Word, which consisted in the Word's voluntary acceptance of the limitations of the incarnation and restraint of Divine power, the starting point of all of his deliberations on the incarnation. *The Word made human experiences his very own by transforming them from within; that which was violent, involuntary, tragically purposeless, and fatal for an ordinary human being was voluntary, soteriologically purposeful, and life-giving in the ministry of the Word. The Word who is above suffering in his own nature suffered by appropriating human nature and obtained victory over suffering.*[76] [emphasis added]

If we read the positions of Tauler and Pannenberg in the light of Cyril's resolution of the problem, the differences between them become less pointed, for they both assume the priority of the self-emptying of the incarnate Christ when they ask, does God suffer?

***

Returning now to Tauler's sermon, he next introduces the three stages of the spiritual life.

The first stage, a life of spirituality and virtue, brings us close to God's presence, and in order to attain this, we must turn completely to the wonderful works of God and to the manifestations of the ineffable gifts which overflow from God's hidden goodness. From this derives a state of soul named "jubilatio." The second stage is spiritual poverty, when in a strange manner

God withdraws Himself from the soul, leaving it anguished and denuded. The third stage is the transition into a divinized life, into a union of our created spirit with God's uncreated one. (141)

We attain the first stage, that of jubilation, by reflecting on the wondrous tokens of love which God has so marvelously granted to us in Heaven and on earth; the abundance of favors God has shown to us and to all His creatures; how all nature—verdant and blossoming—is filled with His glory; how He has flooded the whole creation with His unfathomable mercy; and the great gifts He gave to man, how He has sought him out, guided and enriched him; how He invited and taught him and watched over him with patience; how, for our sake He has become man, suffered, and offered His life and soul for us in order to draw us closer to Him than words can express; and how the Most Blessed Trinity has awaited us to share in its eternal joy. When we reflect upon all this with profound love, a great and active joy will be born in us. And whoever reflects on these matters lovingly will be overwhelmed by such interior joy that his feeble body cannot contain it, and it results in a special outburst of joy. Were it not for this outward expression, strange phenomena would occur, such as physical disorders. Thus it is granted to man to taste how sweet the Lord is, and he experiences union with God in a spiritual embrace. So God attracts, invites, and draws man out of himself, from a state of unlikeness into one of likeness. (142)

This first stage is blessed conversion amid unmitigated sweetness; the second, suffering. In stage two Tauler describes a suffering that is so intense that he names it "desolation."

Now for the second stage: When God has drawn a man far away from created things and made him grow from childhood to maturity, when God has fortified him with spiritual sweetness, then he is offered coarser food; for he now is a man and has become of age. For a grown man, a strong diet is whole-some and good; he no longer needs milk and soft bread. An extremely rough path lies ahead of him, dark and lonely, and as he is led through it, God deprives him of everything He had given him before. The man is now left so completely on his own that he knows nothing at all of God; he is brought to such desolation that he wonders whether he was ever on the right path, whether he has a God or not, whether he really exists; he is so strangely afflicted, so deeply afflicted, that he feels that the whole wide world has become too narrow for him. He can neither taste God nor know Him, and since everything else is insufficient, he feels himself hemmed in between two walls with a sword behind him and a sharp spear in front. What is he to do? Both ways are blocked. (142-143)

This second stage is marked by spiritual desolation. There is an impasse. What is to be done?

Let him sit down and say: "Welcome, bitter affliction, full of grace!" To love and to be denied the object of one's love surely would seem worse than any hell, if there could be one on earth. Whatever one could say to such a man would be of no more comfort than a stone. One cannot speak to him of God, and even less of creatures. The stronger his experience of God was before, the stronger and more intolerable is now the bitterness and pain of loss.

But be of good cheer. The Lord is not far away. Cling to the rock of the true and living faith. Your anguish will soon be over, though in this state your soul cannot conceive that this insufferable darkness could ever give way to light. (143)

Tauler teaches that believers must learn to accept spiritual deso-lation, indeed, to welcome it. "Welcome, bitter affliction—full of grace!" The believer must accept affliction, surrendering himself to God. This acceptance, born of faith, is another way to suffer well in union with God. Tauler is echoing Eckhart's definition of suffering (*leiden*) that also provides the unifying theme of this series of meditations: striving for perfect self-surrender. Faith invites believers to see in every circumstance the providential involvement of God's grace. St. Paul was a witness to this grace. He had prayed three times for God to heal his "thorn in the flesh." When he received the Lord's answer ("My grace is sufficient for you, for my power is made perfect in weakness"), he embraced his suffering: "I will all the more gladly boast of my weaknesses, that the power of Christ may rest upon me." (II Cor 12:9)

For Tauler the worst form of suffering for believers is to be cut off from the source of love. "To love and to be denied the object of one's love surely would seem worse than any hell, if there could be one on earth." In our age, replete with genocides, a Christian can scarcely reflect long on these words before he remembers Christ's cry of dereliction: "'Eloi, Eloi, lama sabachthani?'" ("My God, my God, why hast thou forsaken me?") (Ps 22:1; Mk 15:34) Tauler gave this passage prominence in his theology of suffering, always being careful to make it clear that Jesus suffered in His human nature, not in His divine nature. His position is close to that of Thomas Aquinas as summarized by Gilles Emery:

> The Trinitarian dimension of the cross of Christ is indeed present in St. Thomas's reading of the Gospels...[He taught that] the Father offers his Son for us not in separating himself from the Son, but in giving him with the highest impulse of the Holy Spirit: "he inspired in him the will to suffer for us, by filling him with charity."...The charity of Christ on the cross is the plenitude of the gift of the Holy Spirit in person. This charity is indissociable from the *most profound union* of Christ, in his humanity, with the Father; the center of light which illumines the mystery of suffering. For St. Thomas, it is this *unifying charity* of Christ (which unites him so profoundly with his Father) that confers to his sacrifice its complete value. It is also what permits us to understand the theological meaning

of the satisfaction and merit of Christ: he is the Head of the Church, and all graces proceed from him to the members of his Body, by virtue of the mystical union of Christ with his members; that is to say, insofar as "the Head and members are as one mystical person...In the passion of Christ, who saves us by his love, the joy of the Trinity appears, revealing itself in the *mutual love* of the Father and the Son, in order to associate us with this joy.[77] [italics in text]

Thomas, like Tauler, refuses to introduce a tragic contradiction into the mystery of the cross of Christ. Even on the cross Jesus participates in His humanity in the plenitude of love that He shares with the Father and the Holy Spirit. Thomas drew much of this from Heb. 9:14: "How much more shall the blood of Christ, who through the eternal Spirit offered himself without blemish to God, purify your conscience from dead works to serve the living God." I find this line of thinking compelling because it is precisely by means of the suffering of Jesus in His human nature—a human nature the pre-existent Son of God willingly took upon Himself in His self-emptying act of love in obedience to the Father—that the love that is shared within the Trinity is extended to humankind as a whole, making it possible for the redeemed children of God to participate in this love, even and most especially in their own suffering.

Tauler then proceeds to describe the third stage of the spiritual life, namely, divinization:

For when our Lord has prepared a man's soul by such intolerable trials—and they are a better preparation than any pious devotion—He then comes and raises the soul to the highest stage. And here Our Lord gives him new eyes to see and reveals to him the truth. Now the sun rises in bright splendor and lifts the soul above all its former afflictions. Such a person has indeed returned from death to life. He is led out of himself and enters into Him, the Lord. And now God compensates him for all his anguish and heals him of all his wounds. He raises him from a human to a divine mode of being, from sorrow into a divine peace, in which man becomes so divinized that everything which he is and does, God is and does in him. Such a person is raised so far above any natural mode that he truly becomes by grace what God is essentially by nature. In this state, man feels himself lost in God. He neither knows nor feels nor experiences his former self; he knows only God's simple essence. (143)

This divinization of believers happens by grace, just as God possesses divinity by nature. Disciples of Christ retain their creatureliness, even as they are raised into blessed union with the Creator. But this occurs only when they assume their true place in God's plan by embracing a life of utmost humility. We conclude that for Johannes Tauler suffering is seen as an aspect of human life that is a part of faith's pilgrimage on the way to God. Suffering is central to that pilgrimage because God has ordained to redeem the world by the suffering and death of Christ on the cross. The cross signifies the necessity for believers to pass through suffering on the way to God. For Tauler, only those who become nothing by dying to self can reach fulfillment in God. He states:

Beloved, to have attained this state is truly to have reached the deepest depth of humility, for in this state we have been brought to nothing. It surpasses our powers of comprehension, for here we have reached the most perfect knowledge of our own nothingness. Deeper than this we cannot penetrate into the depth of humility, and the deeper we sink, the higher we rise, for height and depth are here identical. And if a man were to fall from such a height back again upon himself, relapsing into human pride, such a fall would be like the fall of Lucifer. (143-144)

MEDITATION IX

THE WAY OF EMPATHY

"If you want to be obedient, serene, and submissive to God, you must also be serene, obedient, and submissive in relation to the created world around you, in a spirit of compassionate yielding, and not in a spirit of busyness. And all this the soul does in silence, resting in its ground, and in a secret, hidden, suffering empathy, enabling it to carry all, to suffer with all...What happens in a truly divinized person, be it in action or silent suffering compassion, happens in the Light and in this Love. Action and compassion stream out of them, manifest because of them, and flow back into them... If you are content in God, you also find rest in nothing but the Oneness and the All." — The Frankfurt Priest

N THIS MEDITATION WE learn about the highest goal that humankind can attain within time: the precious life of Christ. To attain the life of Christ is to attain union with God. To put us in the right frame of mind to attend to this theme, we hear first from Nicholas Cabasilas—Greek theologian, mystic, and contemporary of the Frankfurt Priest—who was separately arriving at similar conclusions in Constantinople. For him, Christ is the Archetype (or Exemplar) for human beings, not chiefly as a model for ethics but as the one through whom we attain union with God:

It was for the new man that human nature was created at the beginning, and for him mind and desire were prepared. Our reason we have received in order that we may know Christ, our desire in order that we might hasten to Him. We have memory in order that we may carry Him in us, since He Himself is the Archetype for those who are created. It is not the old Adam who was the model for the new, but the new Adam for the old, even though it is said that the new Adam was generated according to the likeness of the old (Rom 8:3) because of the corruption which the old Adam initiated. The latter Adam inherited it in order that He might abolish the infirmity of our nature by means of the remedies which He brings....For those who have known him first, the old Adam is the archetype because of our fallen nature. But for Him who sees all things before they exist the first Adam is the imitation of the second...

So then, for all these reasons man strives for Christ by nature, by his will, by his thoughts, not only because of His Godhead which is the goal of all things, but because of his human nature as well. He is the resting place of human desires; He is the food of our thoughts. To love anything besides him or to meditate on it is a manifest aberration from duty and a turning aside from the first principles of our nature.[78]

***

Cabasilas has directed our attention to the Frankfurt Priest's teachings on the subject of the imitation of Christ and the believer's union with God in and through Jesus Christ. The Frankfurt Priest wrote his *Theologia Germanica* (or *Theologia Deutsch*) many decades after Meister Eckhart did his work, but Eckhart's influence is apparent. You may recall that Eckhart had stressed the importance of stilling the powers of the five senses and the images they form in the mind and falling silent so that God might do His saving work as the eternal birthing of the Word vivifies the soul, bringing new life. In this meditation the Frankfurt Priest revisits Eckhart's teaching on the ground of the soul, both reformulating it and showing how these mystical workings of God shape discipleship. Listen to him:

> [If] we are to yield to God in such stillness we must at the same time be subject to everything, including not only God but also ourselves and all created beings, nothing barred. If you want to be obedient, serene, and submissive to God, you must also be serene, obedient, and submissive in relation to the created world around you, in a spirit of compassionate yielding, and not in a spirit of busyness. *And all this the soul does in silence, resting in its ground, and in a secret, hidden, suffering empathy, enabling it to carry all, to suffer with all.* [emphasis added]
>
> In and during it all the soul takes no recourse to evasion, excuse, resistance, or vengefulness. The newborn soul rather speaks through it all in loving, humble, true compassion: "Father, forgive them; for they know not what they do"…This would be a good path to that which is best for us and a preparation for the highest goal that a man can attain within time. That goal is the precious life of Christ. (88)[79]

I first read this text 24 years ago and I continue to ponder its message today. In an economy of words, the Frankfurt Priest weaves the believer's vocation to surrender her life to God—to yield herself completely to God and all things—together with the ardently desired fruit of this obedience: a virtuous life that strikingly resembles the life of Christ.

We notice first that the Frankfurt Priest urges believers to exchange a frenetic life for one that responds both to God and to created things in a spirit of compassionate yielding. He suggests that the soul do this in silence, resting in its ground, and that all of this involves a kind of imitation of Christ— a walking of the same path that Christ has walked. This peculiar rest yields fruit that only God can grant to the soul: a secret, hidden suffering empathy. This empathy is a form of striving for self-surrender. "And all this the soul does in silence, resting in its ground, and in a secret, hidden, suffering empathy, enabling it to carry all, to suffer with all." This empathy is at work in the ground of the soul and is another way to suffer well in union with God.

This gift from God entails the simultaneity of *rest* and *activity* in the soul and it is the work of God, not man. First, this divine gift grants to the soul the rest to which Jesus refers when He exhorts, "Take my yoke upon you, and learn from me; for I am gentle and humble in heart, and you will find rest for your souls." (Mat 11:29) We human beings often stubbornly refuse to seek this divine rest because of a reluctance to humble ourselves before God. False pride leads us to exalt ourselves above God; we lose our way. When some form of suffering comes along (and inevitably, it will) our grandiose exaltation of ourselves above our Creator is exposed and we are humbled before God. This humility opens the way to the possibility of our finding true rest in God. Second, this secret, hidden, suffering empathy empowers the soul to activity, enabling our spirit to carry all, to suffer with all. It becomes possible for us to turn the other cheek, to love our enemies, and to go the extra mile to aid another. Seeking to imitate Christ, the soul "takes no recourse to evasion, excuse, resistance, or vengefulness…[But] rather speaks through it all in loving, humble, true compassion. 'Father, forgive them; for they know not what they do.'"

The Frankfurt Priest goes on to say that this empathic suffering does not only entail rest and activity in the soul, but includes the ability to show compassion for itself. God's love enables us to have mercy on ourselves as well as on others. He confirms the position of Augustine who says, "…true sacrifices are works of mercy to ourselves or others [that are] done with reference to God."[80] We are invited to have compassion for ourselves and all created things. The mystical eye is opened and is enabled to discern the suffering of all things:

I consider that the sufferings of this time are not worth

comparing with the glory about to be revealed to us. For the creation waits with eager longing for the revealing of the children of God...the creation itself will be set free from its bondage to decay and will obtain the freedom of the glory of the children of God. We know that the whole creation has been groaning in labor pains until now; and not only the creation, but we ourselves... (Rom 8:18, 21-23a)

The creation waits for a revealing. This waiting involves labor pains that imbue the soul with a sure and certain hope. It is not a suffering that simply wrings its hands in shared torment with the sufferer. Rather, the soul joins with Christ as He shares in the sufferings of His members. Hope is anticipatory beatitude. "Faith is the assurance of things hoped for, the conviction of things not seen." (Heb 11:1) Apart from God in Christ, human suffering tends to isolate, constrict, and darken the human spirit. But suffering with Christ can become an occasion for a revelatory glimpse that anticipates the coming fulfillment of God's plan in that Kingdom that has no end. The Christian, spurred on by the theological virtues of faith, hope, and love, is given moments in which this ineffable union breaks through the resistances of the fallen creation: an eternal now. The soul beholds the exquisite beauty and interconnectedness of all things.

In her important book, *Mysticism*, Evelyn Underhill shows that mystical experience can either take the form of a person *looking outward* or *looking inward*. Both types of mysticism can involve suffering in some form or another.

First, she describes the looking outward type of mysticism. Note the presence of an awareness of suffering and sorrow that lies at the heart of things:

Commonly...mystic conversion is a single and abrupt experience, sharply marked off from the long, dim struggles which precede and succeed it. It usually involves a sudden and acute realization of a splendor and adorable reality in the world—or sometimes of its obverse, the divine sorrow at the heart of things—never before perceived. In so far as I am acquainted with the resources of language, there are no words in which this realization can be described.[81]

A little later she goes on to say:

In that remaking of his consciousness which follows upon the "mystical awakening," the deep and primal life which he shares with all creation has been aroused from its sleep. Hence the barrier between human and non-human life, which makes man a stranger on earth as well as in heaven, is done away with. Life now whispers to his life: all things are his intimates, and respond to his fraternal sympathy.[82]

Second, she speaks of an inward looking type of mysticism. This mysticism, which is also conscious of suffering and pain, has to do with the inner life of the soul. It is this inward-looking type of mysticism that has an affinity with the spirituality of the Rhineland Mystics:

Nearly always, this concept, this intimate realization of the divine, has reference to the love and sorrow at the heart of things, the discord between Perfect Love and an imperfect world; whereas the complementary vision of Transcendence strikes a note of rapturous joy....In many conversions to the mystic life, the revelation of an external splendor, the shining vision of the transcendent spiritual world, is wholly absent. The self awakes to that which is within, rather than to that which is without: to the immanent not the transcendent God, to the personal not the cosmic relation. Where those who look out receive the revelation of Divine Beauty, those who look in receive rather the wound of Divine Love.[83]

With these remarks Evelyn Underhill struggles to describe the mystical stirrings in the human soul that we learned about from the

Frankfurt Priest; words fail them both. For the Frankfurt Priest this mystical life belongs to those who participate in the eternal birth of the Son in the ground of the human soul. For him, this inner drama within the soul of each and every believer drives history onward and serves the providence of God. History unfolds within God's inscrutable plan and moves toward fulfillment. Human beings find meaning and significance in history when they accept the Gospel's call to imitate Christ and to live according to the will of God. But the Frankfurt Priest warns Christians about the danger of demanding pat answers to the whys and wherefores of God's mysterious ways:

> You may ask: Seeing that this tree called self-will is so contrary to God and the eternal Will, why has God then created and instated it and placed it in paradise? I answer: Whoever among men and other beings demands to know the hidden counsel of God, desiring to learn why God has done this or that or left this or that undone, that person insists on the same as Adam and the devil.
>
> However long this hankering for disclosure endures, it will never be satisfied, which means, of course, that man is no different from Adam and the devil. For this urge to know God's plan rarely revolves around anything but the pleasure man takes in it and the glory he derives from it, and that is sheer pride.
>
> A truly humble, illumined person does not demand that God disclose His secrets. He does not ask why God does or prevents this or that—and questions in a similar vein. He asks only how to become reduced and surrendering and how the eternal Will might become powerful in him, unhampered by other wills, and how the eternal Will may be fully manifested by and in him. (137)

And in a similar vein the Frankfurt Priest continues:

> I can advance another answer on this matter. One may put

it this way: The noblest and most delightful traits in created beings are knowledge and reason, on the one hand, and will, on the other. These two are intertwined. Where the one is, is also the other. Were it not for these two powers there would be no reasonable creatures, only brutes and brutishness.

It would be like a great emptiness, for God would never receive of His own, there would not be any testing and realization in creation of His own characteristics. But such testing is necessary and part of the work toward perfection.

But now are knowledge and reason created and given together with will. Knowledge and reason are to instruct the will—and themselves—that neither knowing nor willing is on its own or that none of them is or should be a separate self... No, reason and will proceed from the undivided One, they belong to Him, should submit to Him, return to Him, and become reduced to nothing in themselves, that is to say, in their selfdom. (137-138)

***

What characteristics are found in those who submit their reason and will to God, to the Undivided One? The Frankfurt Priest says that such a person possesses three characteristics: peace, humility, and contentment. He is careful to emphasize that each of these aspects of the Christian life includes suffering as an essential part of discipleship.

First, he meditates upon the peace that comes to those who live in Christ:

So we should note and observe the kind of peace Christ left for His disciples in His parting days. He spoke to them and said: "My peace I give to you; not as the world gives do I give to you." For the world's gifts are treacherous.

What kind of peace does Christ mean? He means the inner peace that comes in the midst of hardship, distress, much anguish and misfortune, strain, misery, disgrace, and whatever setbacks there are. Through this peace we become cheerful and patient amid tribulations, just as Christ's dear disciples were— and not they alone but all chosen friends of God and true Christ-followers.

Mark and observe that he who devotes love, diligence, and seriousness to this may well know the true eternal peace that is then the same as God, or as much of God as the creature can possibly receive. (75)

Second, he describes the humility that is a necessary attribute of believers:

Also note this: When true union with God takes place, deep in our being, the inner man is enduringly rooted in that union. But God lets the outer man be moved every which way, in and to matters that are and occur by the rules of earthly life.

This expresses itself in such a way that the outer man says— and, indeed, he is speaking accurately: "I will neither be nor not be, neither live nor die, know nor not know, act nor remain passive, and other such contrary things. But I am prepared in obedience to do what must be and must take place, whether it unfold in inner compassion or in active service."

The outer man has no "wherefore" or real purpose except to fulfill the eternal Will. It becomes truly acknowledged that the inner man shall stand immovable and the outer man must and should be moved. If the inner man has a wherefore in the outer movements of life it is nothing but precisely the duty and obligation ordained by the eternal Will. This is the case where God Himself becomes man, as we see in Christ.

Where man is of this kind and lives from the divine light no spiritual pride appears, no reckless freedom, no undisciplined disposition, only a deep humility and a chastised, reflective, contrite mind. To this life also belong reputable behavior, rectitude, consistency, truthfulness, and everything else pertaining to virtue in human relations. Such things must be there. Where they are not, something has gone wrong with the union...

For whereas this or that particular deed or virtue does not bring about or promote the union, these qualities can, on the other hand, not hinder or obviate it. Only man himself can do this, through his self-will. (97-98)

He speaks again of the humility of those who know that apart from God they are nothing because all good things are rooted in God and come from God:

In a divinized person the godly characteristic is humility, deep in a person's being. Where there is no humility we cannot speak of a divinized person. Christ taught this in words, works, and life.

Humility stems from the inner recognition made in the true Light that being, life, knowledge, wisdom, and power are truly rooted in God, not in the created world. The creature is of itself and has from itself nothing. When it turns away from true Goodness in will and work, nothing is left but wickedness. It is therefore an undeniable truth that the creature as creature is in itself unworthy, has no real claim on anything, no one is indebted to it, neither God nor fellowman. The creature should rightly be surrendered to God's hands, subject to Him.

This is the highest and the most important concern in man's life. (107)

He then connects humility with the true reverence that the believer has for all things:

What is thus—or should be—turned over into God's hands and subject to God must also be surrendered to all creatures and fellow beings (and, briefly, not in terms of outer activity but in terms of inner compassion). If this does not happen the submission is all false. [emphasis added]

From this latter fact, from this article of truth, comes true humility, together with the former article about the allegiance we owe to God. If this were not the truth and the best and highest divine righteousness, Christ would not have taught it in words and fulfilled it in His life. This is where true reverence is born. In truth this is God's way with us: We must, by the power of divine truth and righteousness, be subject to God and all creatures and no single thing and being should be subject to us.

God and all creatures have a right over and claim on the person who abides in God, but that creature has no right to them. I owe debts to all things, no one owes me anything. The divinized creature accepts this compassionately so that he is called to bear all things from others and, when the occasion arises, do all things for others. Out of this grows that spiritual poverty about which Christ spoke: "Blessed are the poor in spirit, for theirs is the kingdom of heaven." Christ taught this in words and fulfilled it in His life. (107-108)

Third, he speaks of Christian contentment in action and in silent suffering compassion. In the quotations that follow, this meditation returns to the theme of a secret, hidden, suffering empathy in the depths of the soul, and beautifully relates it to blessed union with God.

Christian contentment comes in action and silence:

All the concerns about the I, Mine, self, and things connected with them must be utterly lost and surrendered, except, of course, the traits that are necessary for our existence as persons. Thereby we tune into God whose inner-most characteristic is such freedom. What happens in a truly divinized person, be it in action or silent suffering compassion, happens in the Light and in this Love. Action and compassion stream out of them, manifest because of them, and flow back into them.

There is in this person an inner contentment and calm, untroubled by the urge to know more or less, to possess, to live, to die, to be or not to be, and similar strivings—they are all immaterial. (127)

Overcoming the sinful human imprisonment to "the I, Mine, and self" is only possible when believers surrender their attachments to creaturely things. Such surrender allows them to "tune into God" and to walk in God's freedom in "action or silent suffering compassion." He adds that only contentment in God brings true rest in the Oneness and the All:

> You have heard it said that a person who has all his content-ment in God has enough and to spare. This is true. Conversely, he who lets himself be satisfied with particular things in this world derives contentment from nothing pertaining to God. If you are content in God, you also find rest in nothing but the Oneness and the All, which is never this or that particularity. For God is and must be One, He is All and must be All. What exists without being the One is not God. Likewise, what is and is not all and above all can never be God. For God is One and above all. He is All and above all.
>
> He who has his contentment in God is satisfied with and in the One and only in the One as One. And unless a person can see all things as part of the One and one as all things and experience a something and a nothing as the same, he cannot rest content in God. (133)

These words of the Frankfurt Priest convey the spirit of Rhine-land-Flemish spirituality: "If you are content in God, you also find rest in nothing but the Oneness and the All, *which is never this or that particularity*." [emphasis added]. This is suffering in active passivity that involves both detachment from all created things and striving for perfect self-surrender. In the following concluding quotation, the Frankfurt Priest expresses many of the themes of this spirituality:

surrender, obedience, resignation, compassionate sufferance, submission, and stillness. The goal of this spirituality is not mere tranquility, it is union with God without intermediary. In faith the believer seeks to rest contentedly in the Oneness and the All, striving in perfect self-surrender to be submissive to all around him, within the One as the only One:

> But where a person does have such a vision, there comes this satisfaction—and in no other way. Moreover, he who surrenders wholly to God and becomes obedient to Him must have that serene resignation and obedience in compassionate sufferance, which means that he does not resist or defend or evade.
>
> If you are not resigned and submissive to all around you within the One as the only One, you have really not surrendered to and begun to obey God. We can study Christ in this regard. And he who wants to be still in God must have sufferance and be still in Him as the only One, and resist no suffering whatsoever. Christ did this. (133)

MEDITATION X

THE WAY OF UNION

"The first work of Christ...is that God draws the heart, the desires, and all the powers of the soul upward to heaven, calling them to be united with himself and saying spiritually within the heart: "Go out from yourself to me, in accordance with the way in which I am drawing and inviting you." This invitation consists in the shining of Christ, the eternal sun, upon the heart. This causes so much pleasure and joy within the heart and makes the heart open so wide that it can scarcely be closed again. A person is thereby wounded in his heart from within and feels the wound of love...Christ, the true sun, again casts his light and rays upon the wounded, open heart and invites it once more to unity." — John Ruusbroec

THIS STATEMENT SPEAKS OF a peculiar kind of unity, a mystical union with God that believers can enjoy in God. In this final meditation we will try to understand the meaning of this unity. Christians can avoid a common misunderstanding about how we ought to conceive of this unity if our reflections begin with a fundamental dogma of our religion. God is Triune, three Persons—Father, Son, and Holy Spirit. Yet God is One. Thus within the Godhead (quite apart from God's creation) there is a community of Persons. Divine love is not a reality that only becomes realized when God decides to relate to the things of creation. Love is an eternal event within the being of God *as God.* When it comes to suffering, it is crucial that God not be viewed as a solitary, distant, and perfect person who lives in heavenly glory, far removed from his creation. Such a god, as Paul Tillich points out, is not the true God:

> 'Personal God' does not mean that God is a person. It means that God is the ground of everything personal and that he carries within himself the ontological power of personality. He is not a person, but he is not less than personal. It should not be forgotten that classical theology employed the term *persona* for the Trinitarian hypostases but not for God himself. God became a "person" only in the nineteenth century in connection with the Kantian separation of nature ruled by physical law from personality ruled by moral law. Ordinary theism has made God a heavenly, completely perfect person who resides above the world and mankind. The protest of atheism against such a higher person is correct.[84]

John Ruusbroec can help us to reject a misguided theism that makes of God this idealized person. His *Spiritual Espousals* is thoroughly Trinitarian in its theology of suffering, wherein he beautifully describes the Trinitarian basis of our union with God. The words of John Paul II frame our study of this unity, as he too speaks of it in explicitly Trinitarian terms:

> Who is He? The ineffable. Self-existent Being.
> One. Creator of all things.
> And yet, a Communion of Persons.
> In this Communion, a mutual self-giving of the fullness
> Of truth, goodness, and beauty.
> Yet, he spoke to us of himself.
> He spoke, by creating man in his image and likeness.[85]

***

To better understand Ruusbroec's mysticism of love, it is helpful to consider the work of one of the great precursors of Flemish Mysticism, Hadewijch of Antwerp. Although she lived a hundred years before Ruusbroec wrote his *Spiritual Espousals*, she sounded most of the themes that concern him. I can think of no better way to set the course of this final exploration than to briefly sketch her theology of suffering—a theology that directly influenced John Ruusbroec.[86] She too spoke of a "superessential Unity" as a kind of mystical participation in the life of the Trinity of Persons. But what did these two writers mean by this reality?

One thing is certain, and that is that for both Hadewijch and Ruusbroec humility was the paramount Christian virtue, most especially for those who achieve union with God. As Paul Mommaers notes, Hadewijch of Antwerp taught that her attraction to this unity was "a sign of non-full-grownness, and that in mysticism what matters is so to grow up that one is enabled to live wholly other aspects of the being-one with God."[87] In an instructional letter to a fellow Beguine, she writes of the oscillation between the various states of the spiritual life. There is the mystical ecstasy of union with God and the active life of humble service in the world. She writes of this in *Letter 17, Living in the Rhythm of the Trinity*.[88]

(1) Be generous and zealous for every virtue,
But do not apply yourself to any one virtue.

(2) Fail not with regard to a multitude of things,
But perform no particular work.

(3) Have good will and compassion for every need,
But take nothing under your protection.

Mother Columba Hart, O.S.B. points out that these simple lines contain a remarkable Trinitarian theology. Couplet #1 refers to the work of the Holy Spirit; #2 to the work of God the Father; and #3 to the work of the Son. Hart says the first line of each couplet refers to "the outward activity of the Divine Person, in the works attributed to him, while the second verse concerns his unity with the other Divine Persons. Hadewijch would have us shape our life on this rhythm by turning outward in the activity of the virtues, and turning inward again into union with God."[89]

Hadewijch's interpretation of couplet #3, which contains a nascent theology of human suffering, reads as follows:

> Thus his Father engulfed him in himself; this cruel great work ever belongs to the Father. Yet it is the Unity of purest love in the Divinity: so that this Unity is also just with the justice of love and includes this Devotion, this Manhood, and this Power; nor would it have anyone left in need. And it includes one's charity and compassion for those in hell and purgatory; for those unknown to God, or who are known to him but still stray outside his dearest will; and for loving souls, who have more sorrow than all the rest, since they lack what they love. Justice takes up all this into itself. And yet each Person separately has given out what is proper to him.[90]

Important seeds of Ruusbroec's theology of suffering are to be found here. Like Hadewijch, Ruusbroec is concerned to show that the non-ecstatic dimension of Christian living must focus on a life of service to others and on growth in the virtues, even as the soul enjoys a blissful "superessential" union in God.

***

In this final meditation the focus is on John Ruusbroec's description of the believer's mystical union with God. In this life mystical union does not leave suffering behind. For Ruusbroec this union places sacrificial suffering at the very heart of a believer's participation in the *mysterion*. Ruusbroec knew that mystical union with God without intermediary comes at the expense of one's very life. Love requires a believer's death-to-self. In *The Spiritual Espousals* he offers to the Church a Trinitarian mystical theology in which the love of God and human suffering are profoundly interrelated. For him faith begins when the human heart is wounded by Christ. In this life, suffering is the attendant of love:

> The first work of Christ…is that God draws the heart, the desires, and all the powers of the soul upward to heaven, calling them to be united with himself and saying spiritually within the heart: "Go out from yourself to me, in accordance with the way in which I am drawing and inviting you…"
>
> Here the heart opens wide in joy and desire, all the veins dilate, and the powers of the soul stand ready in their desire to fulfill what is called for by God and by the invitation to unity with him. This invitation consists in the shining of Christ, the eternal sun, upon the heart. This causes so much pleasure and joy within the heart and makes the heart open so wide that it can scarcely be closed again. A person is thereby wounded in his heart from within and feels the wound of love. Being wounded by love is both the sweetest feeling and the sharpest pain that anyone can experience and is a sure sign that he will be healed. This spiritual wound causes pleasure and pain at one and the same time. Christ, the true sun, again casts his light and rays upon the wounded, open heart and invites it once more to unity. This renews the wound and all its pangs. (85)[91]

Ruusbroec teaches that the experience of divine love is simultaneous with suffering. "Being wounded by love is both the sweetest feeling and the sharpest pain that anyone can experience and is a sure sign that he will be healed." Sweetness and pain are companions. These odd partners are a sign, a promise, that the sufferer will be healed. The sufferer is being graciously united with God the Father, through the Son, in the power of His Spirit. Ruusbroec is mirroring an insight that he learned from the writings of the mid-13th century Flemish mystic Hadewijch of Antwerp, who writes in one of her letters:

Love stands on trial before none, but all things stand on trial before her. Love borrows from God the power of decision over those she loves. Love will not yield to saints, men here below, Angels in heaven, or earth. She has vanquished the Divinity by her nature. She cries with a loud voice, without stay or respite, in all the hearts of those who love: "Love ye Love!" This voice makes a noise so great and so unheard of that it sounds more fearful than thunder (cf. Apoc. 6:1). *This command is the chain with which Love fetters her prisoners, the sword with which she wounds those she has touched, the rod with which she chastises her children, and the mastership by which she teaches her disciples.*[92] [emphasis added]

For Hadewijch, God's love fetters, wounds, chastises, and teaches His disciples, but love also draws the soul into blessed union with God. Similarly, Ruusbroec holds that this wound of love clears a path to union with God, but he emphasizes that this journey is a painful one because the soul lacks the power to bring this union to fruition:

This interior call and invitation, together with the fact that the creature lifts himself up in readiness to offer himself and all that he can do and nevertheless finds himself unable to reach or obtain this unity, causes a spiritual pain. In other words, when the inmost depths of the heart and the very source of life have been wounded by love and when a person finds himself unable to obtain what he most desires but must ever remain where he does not wish to be, then from this twofold source arises the pain. Here Christ is raised above the topmost part of the mind and casts his divine rays upon the avid desires of the longing heart. This burning radiance dries up and consumes all the moisture, that is, all the powers and forces of human nature. An open and longing heart and the influx of divine rays give rise to an enduring pain. (85-86)

But God does not condemn the soul to suffer endlessly the pain of unmet desire. Ruusbroec speaks of the three modes of meeting God without intermediary:

> Now understand well what follows. The measureless illumination of God which, together with his incomprehensible resplendence, is a cause of all gifts and virtues is the same incomprehensible light which transforms and pervades our spirit's inclination toward blissful enjoyment. It does this in a way which is devoid of all particular form, since it occurs in incomprehensible light. In this light the spirit immerses itself in a rest of pure bliss, for this rest is modeless and fathomless... Here, God's deep calls to deep (Ps 42:7), that is, calls to all who are united with the Spirit of God in blissful love...Thus united—one with the Spirit of God, without intermediary— we are able to meet God with God and endlessly possess our eternal blessedness with him and in him. This most interior way of life is practiced in three manners or modes. (132)

The three modes of meeting God without intermediary are spiritual emptiness, active desire, and simultaneous resting-and-working. He describes each of the modes in turn.

The first mode of meeting God without intermediary is *emptiness*:

> Sometimes a person living the interior life turns within himself in a simple way in accordance with his inclination toward blissful enjoyment. This occurs above and beyond all activity and all virtue, by means of a simple, inward act of gazing in blissful love. Here such a person meets God without intermediary, and an ample light, shining from out of God's Unity, reveals to him darkness, bareness, and nothingness. He is enveloped by the darkness and falls into a modeless state, as though he were completely lost; through the bareness he loses the power of observing all things in their distinctness and

becomes transformed and pervaded by a simple resplendence; in the nothingness all his activity fails him, for he is overcome by the activity of God's fathomless love, while in the inclination of his spirit toward blissful enjoyment he overcomes God and becomes one spirit with him. (cf. I Cor 6:17)[93]

Through this unity in the Spirit of God such a person enters a state of blissful savor and there possesses God's essential being. Being immersed in his own essential being, this person becomes filled with the fathomless delights and riches of God…This is the first mode, which is characterized by emptiness, for it empties a person of all things, lifts him up above all virtues and activities, unites him with God, and provides a firm and stable basis for the most fervent interior exercises… (132-133)

Becoming "one spirit with him" is the greatest blessing that we can receive. That is why in the liturgy the greeting is: "The Lord be with you." And the reply: "And with your spirit."

The second mode of meeting God without intermediary is *active desire*:

At times this interiorly fervent person turns to God in a way characterized by desire and activity, so that he might give God glory and honor and might offer him both himself and all his works, letting them be consumed in the love of God. At such times he meets God with intermediary, namely, the intermediary of the gift of savorous wisdom. This gift is the ground and source of all virtue, for it urges and moves every good person toward virtue in accordance with the degree of love. It sometimes touches an interior person so deeply and enkindles his love so intensely that all God's gifts and all that God can bestow apart from himself are too small and unsatisfying and serve only to increase his restlessness. Such a person has an interior perception or feeling in the ground of his being, where all virtues have their beginning and end, where with ardent desire he offers God all these virtues, and where love has its abode. Here the hunger and thirst of love are so great that he surrenders himself at every moment and is unable to work any further, but rather transcends his activity and comes to naught in love…Though living he dies; though dying he comes back to life. In this way the yearning hunger and thirst of love are constantly renewed within him. (133-134)

For Ruusbroec, true spiritual desire is directed beyond all of God's gifts and everything that God can bestow apart from Himself, to union with God without intermediary. Short of this union, the human spirit will continue to hunger and thirst for God without rest:

This is the second mode, one which is characterized by desire. In it, love stands in a state of likeness and yearningly desires to be united with God. This mode is more honorable and more beneficial to us than the first since it is the cause of the first, for no one can enter a state of rest transcending activity unless he has previously loved in a way characterized by desire and activity. For this reason God's grace and our active love must both precede and follow, that is, must be practiced both before and after, for without works of love we cannot merit or attain God nor can we retain what we have gained by means of works of love. Therefore no one should be empty of activity if he is master of himself and can give himself to the works of love. But whenever a good person lingers somewhat over any of God's gifts or over any creature, he will be hindered in this most interior exercise, for it is a hunger which cannot be satisfied by anything or anyone except God alone. (134)

Clearly for Ruusbroec, God's grace and good works are intimately linked in Christian discipleship. His form of Christian mysticism does not lead to social quietism or passive self-absorption. He guards against such dangers by providing a holistic vision that emphasizes that an active life of service to others is central to the life of a Christian. Note the intimate relation that Ruusbroec draws between the first two modes of meeting God without intermediary—the modes of emptiness and active desire. Thomas Merton, the Trappist monk and mystic, also reflects on this close relationship between emptiness and desire when he speaks of the role of the "simple intention" of the believer:

> Simple intention is a rare gift of God. Rare because it is poor. Poverty is a gift that few religious people really relish. They want their religion to make them at least spiritually rich, and if they renounce all things in this world, they want to lay hands not only on life everlasting but, above all, on the "hundred-fold" promised to us [in Jesus' parable] even before we die.
>
> Actually, that hundredfold is found in the beatitudes, the first of which is poverty.
>
> Our intention cannot be completely simple unless it is completely poor. It seeks and desires nothing but the supreme poverty of having nothing but God. True, anyone with a grain of faith realizes that to have God and nothing else besides is to have everything in Him. But between the thought of such poverty and its actualization in our lives lies the desert of emptiness through which we must travel in order to find Him.
>
> With a right intention, you quietly face the risk of losing the fruit of your work. With a simple intention you renounce the fruit before you even begin. You no longer even expect it. Only at this price can your work also become a prayer.[94]

Merton then connects simple intention with the healing balm of God's grace:

> A simple intention is a perpetual death in Christ. It keeps our life hidden with Christ in God. It seeks its treasure nowhere except in heaven. It prefers what cannot be touched,

counted, weighed, tasted, or seen. But it makes our inner being open out, at every moment, into the abyss of divine peace in which our life and actions have their roots.

A right intention aims only at right action.

But even in the midst of action, a simple intention, renouncing all things but God alone, seeks Him alone. The secret of simple intention is that it is content to seek God and does not insist on finding Him right away, knowing that in seeking Him it has already found Him. Right intention knows this too, but not by experience, and therefore it obscurely feels that seeking God is still not enough.

Simple intention is a divine medicine, a balm that soothes the powers of the soul wounded by inordinate self-expression. It heals our actions in their secret infirmity. It draws our strength to the hidden summit of our being, and bathes our spirit in the infinite mercy of God. It wounds our souls in order to heal them in Christ, for a simple intention manifests the presence and action of Christ in our hearts.[95]

***

The third mode of meeting God without intermediary is *resting and working:*

From these first two modes [i.e. emptiness and active desire] there arises a third, which is an interior life in accordance with righteousness. You should understand that God comes ceaselessly to us both with intermediary and without intermediary and calls us both to blissful enjoyment and to activity in such a way that the one will not be hindered by the other but rather constantly strengthened by it. An interior person therefore possesses his life in these two ways, that is, in rest and activity, and in each he is whole and undivided, for he is completely in God when he blissfully rests and is completely in himself when he actively loves. He is exhorted and called by God at all times to renew both his rest and his activity, and his spirit's righteousness wishes to pay at each instant whatever God asks of it. For this reason the spirit turns inward both actively and with blissful enjoyment each time it experiences God's sudden illumination. In this way it is constantly renewed in all the virtues and becomes more deeply immersed in blissful rest, for each time God bestows something on us he gives himself as well as his gifts, while in each of its inward movements the spirit gives itself as well as all its works. By means of God's simple illumination and the spirit's inclination to be blissfully immersed in love, the spirit is united with God and is ceaselessly transported into a state of rest. In addition, by means of the gifts of understanding and of savorous wisdom, it is actively touched and at all times enlightened and enkindled in love. (134-135)

The third mode of meeting God is a life in which, by God's grace, a believer is in full possession of his or her interior life:

To a person in this state there is spiritually revealed and held out before him all that one could desire. He is hungry and thirsty, for he sees angelic food and heavenly drink; he works intensely in love, for he sees his rest; he is a pilgrim and sees his fatherland; he strives for victory in love, for he sees his crown. Consolation, peace, joy, beauty, riches, and everything else that brings delight is revealed in God to the enlightened reason without measure in spiritual likenesses. Through this revelation and God's touch love remains active, for this righteous person has established for himself a truly spiritual life in both rest and activity; such a life will continue forever, though after this present life it will be transformed into a higher state. (135)

***

Near the end of his treatise, Ruusbroec describes the believer's mystical union with God. Paradoxically, it is precisely at the moment of this blessed union that this "loving as Christ loves" (John 15:12) requires the greatest sacrifice of the believer: death to self.

> All the richness which is in God by nature is something which we lovingly possess in God—and God in us—through the infinite love which is the Holy Spirit. In this love a person savors all that he can desire. *By means of this love we have died to ourselves* [emphasis added] and through a loving immersion of ourselves have gone out into a state of darkness devoid of particular form. There the spirit is caught up in the embrace of the Holy Trinity and eternally abides within the superessential Unity in a state of rest and blissful enjoyment...(148)

Death "by means of this love" is the human creature's acceptance of dying to self, which is already undergone in Holy Baptism: "Do you not know that all of us who have been baptized into Christ Jesus were baptized into his death? We were buried therefore with him by baptism into death, so that as Christ was raised from the dead by the glory of the Father, we too might walk in newness of life." (Rom 6:3-4) For Christians, death "by means of this love" is not a tragedy. It is a work of divine grace because it is the death of the "old Adam." Out of this death comes the gracious embrace of the Holy Trinity as the soul "abides within the superessential Unity in a state of rest and blissful enjoyment." This superessential Unity is the believer's blessed participation in the life of the Holy Trinity.

We began this meditation by stating that the goal was to understand the nature of what Ruusbroec calls "superessential unity." The concept can lead to confusion, and even in Ruusbroec's day there were those who questioned the orthodoxy of some of his statements about union with God without intermediaries. In *The Little Book of Clarification* Ruusbroec addressed these concerns. His comments help to deepen our understanding of "superessential unity."[96]

In the first place, I say that *all good persons are united with God through an intermediary.* [emphasis added] This intermediary is God's grace, together with the sacraments of the holy Church, the divine virtues of faith, hope, and love, and a virtuous life in accordance with God's commandments…(253)

Whenever a person who lives in this way raises himself up with the entirety of his being and with all the powers and devotes himself to God with a living and active love, then he feels that his love—in its very ground where it begins and ends—is blissful and devoid of any ground. If he then wishes to penetrate further into this blissful love with his active love, all the powers of his soul will give way and will have to suffer and endure that penetrating truth and goodness which is God himself. In the same way that the air is pervaded with the radiance and warmth of the sun or a piece of iron is penetrated by fire, so that with the fire it does the work of fire, burning and giving light just as fire does…and yet *each retains its own nature* [emphasis added] for the fire does not become iron, nor the iron fire, but the union is without intermediary, for the iron is within the fire and the fire within the iron…(259)

Even though the union between the loving spirit and God is without intermediary, there is nevertheless a great difference, *for the creature does not become God nor does God become the creature* [emphasis added], just as I said concerning the iron…(260)

Nevertheless, *the creature does not become God, for this union occurs through grace and through a love which has been turned back to God.* [emphasis added] For this reason the creature experiences in his inward vision a difference and distinction between himself and God. Even though the union is without intermediary, the manifold works which God performs in heaven and on earth are hidden from the spirit. (265)

These statements clarify Ruusbroec's concept of union without intermediary. But perhaps the clearest and therefore most helpful statement on the matter is the following:

> This bliss is essential to God alone; to all spirits it is superessential for no created being can be one with God's being and have its own being perish. For if that happened, the creature would become God, and this is impossible, for God's essential being can neither decrease nor increase and can have nothing taken away from it or added to it. (265-266)

By striving for perfect self-surrender, the believer suffers death to self by means of divine love and enjoys "superessential" union with God—all the while remaining a creature of God.

***

Finally, we take a step back to catch a glimpse of the basic vision and overarching theme of Rhineland-Flemish spirituality. Louis Bouyer summarizes it this way: "For each of us, everything comes back to becoming such in ourselves as we eternally are as God sees each of us in his Son, for all eternity."[97]

John Ruusbroec bears out Bouyer's summary statement and provides a crowning vision that brings his treatise, and our series of meditations, to a fitting close:

> In this same [superessential] Unity, considered now as regards its fruitfulness, the Father is in the Son and the Son in the Father, while all creatures are in them both. This is beyond the distinction of Persons, for here we can only make distinctions of reason between fatherhood and sonship in the living fecundity of the divine nature.
> This is the origin and beginning of an eternal going forth and an eternal activity which is without beginning, for it is a

beginning without beginning. Since the almighty Father has perfectly comprehended himself in the ground of his fruitfulness, the Son, who is the Father's eternal Word, goes forth as another Person within the Godhead. Through this eternal birth all creatures have gone forth eternally before their creation in time. God has thus seen and known them in himself—as distinct in his living ideas and as different from himself, though not different in every respect, for all that is in God is God. (148-149)

In the end he rests everything upon the grace of God and prayer:

That we might blissfully possess the essential Unity and clearly contemplate the Unity in the Trinity—may the divine love grant us this, for it turns no beggar away. Amen. Amen. (152)

CONCLUSION

The Rhineland-Flemish Mystics shine the light of Christ on every form of human suffering, whether it is suffering of mind, body, or spirit. They show that Christ not only brings consolation to the sufferer, He also brings new life. Faith—human participation in the eternal birth of the Word in the ground of the soul—revivifies the human spirit and transforms the experience of suffering. Thus a believer knows that any suffering that he or she undergoes, whether it is deserved or undeserved, will take place in union with Christ.

CHRISTIAN ORTHODOXY HAS NEVER been much interested in theological innovation, but in every age Christians seek to behold and pass on the good news of Jesus Christ in ever new ways while remaining faithful to the original Apostolic witness. In line with this faithful tradition, we have seen how the Rhineland-Flemish theology of human suffering manifests the believer's blessed participation in God's redemptive act of suffering-love in Jesus Christ—who as the resurrected Lord has become *Pneuma* (life-giving Spirit). This is a distinctive medieval theology that can enrich the practical ministry of the Church today. The subject of suffering is by its very nature intense, at times dark; yet this theology is imbued with a joy that is always new, directing hearts and minds to the Gospel—hidden and revealed. The wellspring of this theology is the secret, hidden, saving activity of the Word of God. And for the Rhineland-Flemish Mystics, the word that speaks in the depths (or ground) of the human soul to engage, assuage, and ultimately to abolish suffering is the living Word: Jesus Christ.

From these meditations we glean that in Rhineland-Flemish spirituality suffering does not refer first and foremost to the physical pain, mental anguish, or loss and grief of the sufferer. To say this is not to ignore these common forms of suffering; far from it. They are, of course, true forms of suffering. But another aspect of suffering is given precedence over them. This is suffering that is viewed, in a deeper spiritual sense, as *a person's trusting surrender, in a posture of inner passivity that waits expectantly for God to do His saving work in the soul.* It follows from this that suffering is not, as is commonly assumed, simply negative; in fact, it can be supremely positive. Indeed, due to sin and the disordered state of the world, it is God's will that suffering play a central role in Christian discipleship, mirroring the cross of Christ. Out of this suffering comes newness of life: salvation. Suffering, in its essence, involves the stilling of the five senses and the images they form in the mind and falling silent in active passivity so that God might do His saving work in the ground of the soul. Far from being something abhorrent that should be avoided at all costs, it turns out that suffering often plays a vital, life-giving role in a believer's blessed conversion to life in God: "Not my will, but Thy will be done."

The books and sermons of these theologians reveal ten themes that teach us the profound truth that suffering (understood as striving for perfect self-surrender) plays a decisive role in Christian life. In brief, here is a summary of the *Ten Ways to Suffer Well in Union with God.*

Meditations I-V explored the revelatory interaction between the twin mysteries of human suffering and divine love. (I) Surrender: Stilling the mind and the five senses that form images in the mind, the believer suffers, striving for perfect self-surrender in order to hear the life-giving Word of God in the depths of the soul. Surrender is the principal theme that unites all of the themes of this theology. (II) Pray: Turning away from created things, the believer patiently surrenders all human striving, waiting for God to bring life and light. Closely related to this surrender is the prayerful carrying of all concerns and burdens to the Source in the ground of the soul. (III) Yield: Central to the life of Christian discipleship is the vocation to imitate Christ and His cross-shaped life. Believers must yield to God's call to walk down the right path— the path that leads to the true end of human life. That path is the perfect life of Christ. (IV) Imitate: Resisting the temptation to dream triumphantly of a life of discipleship that is filled only with sweetness and light, the Christian willingly shares in the suffering humanity of Christ in order to win, in God's good time, a share in His divinity. (V) Co-suffer: Compassion is a wounding of the heart which love extends to all without distinction. This wound cannot be healed as long as anyone still suffers, for to compassion alone, above all other virtues, God has commended sorrow and suffering. For this reason Christ says, "Blessed are the sorrowing, for they shall be consoled." (Mt 5:4)

Meditations VI-X showed how the suffering love of Christ transforms human suffering when it is undergone in union with God. (VI) Participate: Clinging in faith to the knowledge that God is One, a believer freely suffers in the moment of grace, receiving new life. Whatever a believer suffers for God's sake is suffered before God's face, in God. What more could a sufferer want? (VII) Love: Rising out of the ensnaring foulness of temporal delights, the soul reawakens to its true vocation and the stubborn human demand for a theodicy—a justification of God in the face of suffering—is redirected by grace into the sphere of divine love. (VIII) Accept: Embracing all suffering (deserved or undeserved) as coming from the hand of God, the believer declares: "Welcome, bitter affliction, full of grace." Then God comes and raises the soul to the highest stage, leading the believer out of himself and into God. (IX) Empathize: If you want to be obedient, serene, and submissive to God, you must also be obedient, serene, and submissive to the created world around you, in a spirit of compassionate yielding. All this the soul does in silence, resting in its ground, and in a secret, hidden suffering empathy. If you are content in God, you will find rest in nothing but the Oneness and the All. (X) Unite: God summons us, "Go out from yourself to me." Christ casts His light upon the wounded, open heart, and invites it once more to unity. Dying to self by means of divine love, the believer's spirit is caught up in the embrace of the Trinity, abiding in the superessential unity.

In conclusion, it is clear that the *Ten Ways to Suffer Well in Union with God* confirms that suffering lies at the heart of the Christian Mystery, which in its fullness encompasses a joyous passage of the believer from death to life through the cross to the resurrection that was once and for all accomplished in Christ. This theology of suffering, so rich in wise guidance for Christian living, can serve as a reminder to believers to be attentive to the mystical workings of God's Spirit in their own lives and in the lives of the people with whom they live and to whom they minister. Believers are also reminded to celebrate without ceasing the wondrous depth of God's saving communion with all who suffer in Christ. Although they themselves were not in a position to fully grasp it, we today are graced by the beautiful theology of suffering that comes to us from Meister Eckhart (the Philosopher of Faith), Johannes Tauler (the Tender Pastor), the Frankfurt Priest (the Admonishing Teacher), Henry Suso (the Prophet of Wisdom), and John Russbroec (the Spiritual Director).

The Rhineland-Flemish Mystics shine the light of Christ on every form of human suffering, whether it is suffering of mind, body, or spirit. They show that Christ not only brings consolation to the sufferer, but He also brings new life. Faith—human participation in the eternal birth of the Word in the ground of the soul—revivifies the human spirit and transforms the experience of suffering. Thus a believer knows that any suffering that he or she undergoes, whether it is deserved or undeserved, will take place in union with Christ. In this mystical union the sufferer is united with the Father, through the Son, in the power of the Spirit. And this union means everything to the sufferer because "the last Adam became a life-giving spirit"[98] and to be "one spirit with him"[99] is to be truly alive.

+

AFTERWORD

YOU ARE NOT ABOVE YOUR MASTER,
WHO SUFFERED AND DIED FOR YOU.

THIS BOOK GREW OUT of events in my personal faith story and from my discovery of the Rhineland-Flemish theology of suffering. It was fed by my desire to better understand the peace of God which surpasses all understanding. A full measure of that peace was given to me as I stood at the grave of my young friend, Bobby Laxton, almost 50 years ago.

I still remember clearly those first difficult days in the summer of 1967 after the crash that took the lives of Bobby and the other boys in that car, Randy, Ron, and Peter. One memory in particular stands out. Because they were Catholics the joint funeral was held in the cathedral, and their caskets were all lined up in a nice neat row. But the orderly scene seemed contrived to me. What I saw was chaos. At some deep level in my spirit, I made a decision: "I refuse to live in a world that crushes the beauty of the rose unfolding; I will fly away." Although I never lost my faith, out of faintness of heart I drew back at the thought of living in a world in which suffering and death hold such sway. Let us call this decision my "great refusal."

Fast forward 25 years to 1992. At age 43 I stood before Bobby's grave for the first time since his burial. And as I prayed, the protective edifice I had built around my "great refusal" crumbled like the fated walls of Jericho. It is true: Faith moves mountains.

It was five Christians from the 14th century who helped me the most to integrate this saving moment into my religious beliefs. How did this happen? I have a short answer and a long one.

The short answer is that their theological perspectives allowed me to see that just as my "great refusal" had occurred at some deep level in my spirit, so also did God's Spirit act in the deepest depths of my soul, revivifying my life. My "great refusal" was no match for the Word of God; my resistance collapsed.

The long answer is given in the pages of this book, in the theology of suffering that I retrieved from the books and sermons of these theologians. Like the discerning guidance that comes from a good spiritual director, their message spoke to me loud and clear:

Freed from the suffocating narrowness of a hunkered-down existence, Christ wants your life to open out to the fullness of life in union with God. Embrace life in our world, a world that does indeed often crush the tender rose of budding youth. Remember that you are not above your Master, who suffered and died for you. He calls upon you, and all of His chosen ones, to suffer, striving for perfect self-surrender in spiritual detachment from the things of this world. Pray, yield, imitate, co-suffer, participate, love, accept, and empathize—in blessed union with God.

Today my thoughts seldom linger for long on my experience at the cemetery. But my reflections do often turn—aided by the theology of the Rhineland-Flemish Mystics—to the inner life of faith that is hidden in the depths of the human soul, to the mystery of time and eternity, to the indescribable beauty of a solitary human life, to the unfathomable love that moved God to create human beings as creatures who find their rest in Him alone, and to the miraculous power of the Gospel that is able to bring newness of life and divine peace into the human soul.

ENDNOTES

1   E.g. Wis. 8:2, Wis. 18:14-15, John 1:9-13, Eph. 1:4, Ps 36:9, Mat. 5:8, I John 3:1-2, Gal. 2:20, Col. 1:12-20, 24-27 (esp. 1:24), Col 1:28-2:3, Eph 1:5-10 (esp. 9-10), Ps. 42:7a, I Cor 6:17, I Cor 15:45, Rom 8:9b-11, Mat. 25:6, I Cor. 2:10-16 (esp. 2:11b), John 14:23, and Mat 11:25.

2   Servais Pinckaers, O.P., *The Sources of Christian Ethics*, translated from the third edition by Sr. Mary Thomas Noble, (Washington D.C.: The Catholic University of America, 1995), 32.

3   **Meister Eckhart** (1260-1328) was born in Thuringia, Germany. He joined the Dominicans and in 1275 was sent to Cologne where he probably studied for a time under Albert the Great (who died in 1280). Although he also wrote works of scholastic theology in Latin, his best known works are more than a hundred sermons and his *Book of Divine Comfort*, both published in his vernacular Middle High German tongue. In English translation see the marvelous *The Complete Mystical Works of Meister Eckhart*, Translated and Edited by Maurice O'C. Walshe. Revised, with a Foreword by Bernard McGinn (New York: A Herder and Herder Book, The Crossroads Publishing Company, 2009). See also *Meister Eckhart: The Essential Sermons*, Edited by Bernard McGinn (New York: Paulist Press, 1981). *The Book of*

Divine Comfort is studied in Meditation VI.

4 Page references in the body of the text for this first meditation are from Eckhart, *The Complete Mystical Works of Meister Eckhart*. Italics are in the original text.

5 *Johannes Tauler, Sermons*, The Classics of Western Spirituality, Trans. by Mary Shady with an Introduction by Josef Schmidt. Preface by Alois Haas (New York: Paulist Press, 1985), 32.

6 See Eckhart's essay, "On Detachment" in Eckhart, *The Complete Mystical Works of Meister Eckhart*, 566-575.

7 Hans Urs von Balthasar, *The Glory of the Lord, A Theological Aesthetics, Volume VII: Theology: The New Covenant*, Translated by Brian McNeil C.R.V. and Edited by John Riches (San Francisco: Ignatius Press, 1989), 405.

8 Balthasar, *The Glory of the Lord, Vol. VII*, 405.

9 Balthasar, *The Glory of the Lord, Vol. VII*. 405.

MEDITATION II

10 This quotation and my brief discussion of *nous* and *pneuma* that follows draw heavily from Gerhard Ebeling, *The Nature of Faith* (London: Collins, 1961), 101-102.

11 Jerome A. Miller, *The Way of Suffering, A Geography of Crisis* (Washington D.C.: Georgetown University Press, 1988), 2.

12 **Johannes Tauler** (1300-1366) was a Dominican preacher and pastor from Strasbourg who for many years lived in Basle. His sermons have been read by both Catholics and Protestants throughout the centuries. See John Tauler, *Johannes Tauler, Sermons*, The Classics of Western Spirituality (New York: Paulist Press, 1985). Also, John Tauler, *Spiritual Conferences*, trans. and ed. by Eric Colledge and Sister M. Jane, O.P. (Rockford: Tan Books and Publishers, Inc. 1978)

13 Tauler in Steven Ozment, *Homo Spiritualis* (Leiden: E. J. Brill, 1969), 25-26. Unless otherwise noted, italics are in the original text.

14 Tauler, *Spiritual Conferences*, 143-144. This translation renders the

Middle High German word *grunt* as "depths" rather than using the word "ground. "

15 Tauler in Ozment, *Homo Spiritualis*, 23.

16 Tauler in Ozment, *Homo Spiritualis*, 23-24.

17 Tauler in Ozment, *Homo Spiritualis*, 23.

18 Hans Urs von Balthasar in *The Glory Of The Lord, A Theological Aesthetics, Volume I: Seeing the Form*, Translated by Erasmo Leiva-Merikakis. Ed. by Joseph Fessio S. J. and John Riches (San Francisco: Ignatius Press, 1982), 156.

19 Quoted in "The Spirituality of Meister Eckhart and Its Implications for Christian Life Today" in *Spiritual Life*, 2010. p. 15.

20 Tauler, *Spiritual Conferences*, 98.

21 Tauler, *Spiritual Conferences*, 61.

22 Tauler, *Spiritual Conferences*, 82-83.

23 Henri de Lubac, *The Mystery of the Supernatural*, tr. R. Sheed (New York: Herder & Herder, 1967), 69-70.

24 Romano Guardini, *The Lord* (Chicago: Henry Regnery Company, 1954), 506-507.

25 *Luther's Works, Volume 25, Lectures on Romans, Glosses and Scholia*, Translated by Walter G. Tillmanns and Jacob A. O. Preus. Hilton C. Oswald, Editor (Saint Louis: Concordia Publishing House, 1972), 286-287.

26 Martin Luther, *Luther's Works, Volume 25, Lectures on Romans*, 287-288.

27 Heiko A. Oberman, *Luther: Man Between God and the Devil* (London: Yale University Press, 1989), 180.

28 This summary paraphrases Sevais Pinckaers' "Aquinas on the Dignity of the Human Person" in *Pinckaers Reader*, (Catholic University of America Press, 2005), 157-156.

29 Tauler, *Johannes Tauler, Sermons*, 164.

30 Tauler, *Johannes Tauler, Sermons*, 164.

31 Tauler, *Johannes Tauler, Sermons*, 164.

32 Throughout this third meditation the page references in the body of the text are taken from The (anonymous) Frankfurt Priest, *The Theologia Germanica of Martin Luther, The Classics of Western Spirituality,* Translation, Introduction and Commentary by Bengt Hoffman (New York: Paulist Press, 1980).

33 **The Frankfurt Priest**, anonymous author of *Theologia Germanica or Theologia Deutsch*, was a priest and warden of the Teutonic Order in Frankfurt, Germany. His mystical theology departs from that of the three Dominicans—Eckhart, Tauler and Suso—with regard to his Augustinian doctrine of sin, yet his little book exudes the spirit of Rhineland-Flemish spirituality. The book was written some time between the years 1350 and 1390. See also the same book recently published with the title: *The Book of the Perfect Life,* translation and with an Introduction and Notes by David Blamires (Walnut Creek: AltaMira Press. 2003).

34 Dietrich von Hildebrand, *The Heart, An Analysis of Human and Divine Affectivity* (South Bend, Indiana: St. Augustine Press, 2007), 115.

35 "Pastoral Constitution on the Church in the World Today," 22. Second Vatican Council. *Decrees of the Ecumenical Councils, Vol I, From Trent to Vatican II*, Edited by Norman P. Tanner (Washington D.C.: S.J. Sheed and Ward, 1990), 1081.

36 Wolfhart Pannenberg, *Systematic Theology, Volume 2,* Translated by Geoffrey W. Bromiley (Grand Rapids: William B. Eerdmans, 1994), 375.

37 Paul L. Gavrilyuk, *The Suffering of the Impassible God, The Dialectics of Patristic Thought* (Oxford: Oxford University Press, 2004), 71.

38 Hans Urs von Balthsar, *The Glory of the Lord, Seeing the Form, Vol. I* (San Francisco: Ignatius Press and Crossroad, 1982), 263. Cf. Heb 5:5-10.

39 *Leisure, The Basis Of Culture*, Introduction by Roger Scruton. New translation by Gerald Malsbary (South Bend, Indiana: St. Augustine's Press, 1998), 28.

40 Wolfhart Pannenberg, *Systematic Theology, Vol 2* (Grand Rapids: Eerdmans Publishing Company, 1994), 379.

41 **Henry Suso** (1300-1366) was a Dominican who studied in Cologne. Eckhart was his teacher and spiritual director for a time. He is remembered today chiefly for his Latin work, *Wisdom's Watch Upon the Hours*, which we study in Meditation VII. He also wrote in his vernacular German *The Little Book of Truth, The Little Book of Eternal Wisdom*, and *The Life of the Servant*. Tauler and Suso were friends as well as leaders of the lay movement known as the Friends of God. See also *Bl. Henry Suso, Wisdom's Watch Upon The Hours*, Translated by Edmond Colledge (Washington D.C.: The Catholic University of America Press, 1994). And *Henry Suso, The Exemplar, with Two German Sermons*, The Classics of Western Spirituality, Translated, Edited, and Introduction by Frank Tobin. Preface by Bernard McGinn (New York: Paulist Press, 1989).

42 The page references in the body of the text in this meditation are from *Henry Suso, The Exemplar with Two German Sermons* (New York: Paulist Press, 1989).

43 *Catechism of the Catholic Church, Second Edition* (Libreria Editrice Vaticana, 1994), # 2842. Hereafter cited as CCC.

44 See the comments of Donald F. Duclow on page 81 on the subject of the Rhineland Mystics' understanding of the Oneness of God and its significance for Christian discipleship.

45 John Ruusbroec, *John Ruusbroec: The Spiritual Espousals and Other Works*, Introduction and Translation by James A. Wiseman, O.S.B. (New York: Paulist Press, 1985), 60. **John Ruusbroec**

(1293-1381) was a priest in Brussels for 26 years before entering a long period of contemplation and writing in the wooded solitude of Groenendaal. *The Spiritual Espousals* is his Flemish masterpiece. He sent a copy of his *Spiritual Espousals* to the Friends of God in Strasbourg in 1350.

46 Romano Guardini, *The Lord*, p. 385.

47 John Ruusbroec, *The Spiritual Espousals and Other Works*, pp. 59-60.

48 C.S. Lewis, *The Four Loves* (New York: Harcourt Brace Modern Classic, 1988), 121.

49 Alasdair MacIntyre, *Rational Dependent Animals, Why Human Beings Need the Virtues* (Chicago: Open Court, 1999), 125.

50 Grahame Greene, *The Power and the Glory* (New York: Penguin Books, 2003), 82-83.

51 The quote is from Louis Bouyer, *The Christian Mystery, From Pagan Myth to Christian Mysticism*, and Translated by Illtyd Trethowan (Edinburgh: T&T Clark, 1990), 225.

52 From "Lincoln's Sacramental Language" by Andrew Delbanco, in *Our Lincoln, New Perspectives on Lincoln and His World*, edited by Eric Fonner (New York: W.W. Norton and Company, Inc. 2008), 199.

53 Quoted in Hans Urs von Balthasar, *Mysterium Paschale, The Mystery of Easter*, Translated with an Introduction by Aidan Nichols, O.P. (San Francisco: Ignatius Press, 2005), 104.

54 Balthasar, *Mysterium Paschale*, 104.

55 *Salvifici Dolores, On the Christian Meaning of Human Suffering* (Boston: Pauline Books and Media, 1984), 45-46.

56 Johann Gerhard, *Theological Commonplaces, On the Person and Office of Christ* (1625), Translated by Richard J. Dinda (Saint Louis: Concordia Publishing House, 2009), 201-202.

57 Gregory the Great, in Henri De Lubac, *Catholicism, Christ and the Common Destiny of Man*, Translated by Lancelot C. Sheppard and Sister Elizabeth Englund, OCD (San Francisco: Ignatius Press, 1988), 364, footnote 22.

58 The page references in the body of the text in Meditation VI are from Eckhart, *The Complete Mystical Works of Meister Eckhart* (New York: A Herder and Herder Book. The Crossroads Publishing Company. 2009). Italics are in the original texts.

59 This is from a sermon on Wisdom 18:14 in Eckhart, *The Complete Mystical Works of Meister Eckhart*, 33.

60 John Paul II, *Salvifici Dolores, On the Christian Meaning of Human Suffering*, 27-28.

61 Eckhart, *The Complete Mystical Works of Meister Eckhart*, Note 61, 55.

62 "My Suffering Is God: Meister Eckhart's Book of Divine Consolation" in *Theological Studies* 44 (1983), p. 576.

63 Donald F Duclow, "My Suffering Is God" in *Theological Studies* 44 (1983), p. 575.

64 *Rational Dependent Animals, Why Human Beings Need the Virtues*, Alastair MacIntyre (Chicago and La Salle, Illinois: Open Court, 1999), 1-2.

65 *Dialogues Concerning Natural Religion*, ed. Nelson Pike (Indianopolis: Bobbs-Merrill, 1970), part 10, 88.

66 The page references in the body of the text for Meditation VII are from Suso's, *Wisdom's Watch Upon the Hours* (Washington D.C.: The Catholic University of America, 1994).

67 *Salvifici Dolores*, 17-18.

68 John Chrysostom, Homily 24.2; Patrologia graeca 61: 200. Quoted in Enrico Mazza, *The Origins of the Eucharistic Prayer* (Collegeville: The Liturgical Press, 1995), 76, note 28.

69 John D. Zizioulas, *Being As Communion, Studies in Personhood and the Church*, Foreword by John Meyendorff (Crestwood, New York: St. Vladimir's Seminary Press, 1985), 94.

70 Edgar Lee Masters, *Spoon River Anthology, An Annotated Edition.*

Edited and with an Introduction and annotations by John E. Hall-was (Urbana and Chicago: University of Illinois Press, 1992), 329.

71 The three quotes that follow are from *Henry Suso, The Exemplar with Two German Sermons* (New York: Paulist Press, 1989), 247-249 various, from *The Little Book of Eternal Wisdom.*

MEDITATION VIII

72 John Paul II, *Salvifici Dolores*, 28.

73 The page references in the body of the text for Meditation VIII refer to this sermon, which is taken from Tauler, *Johannes Tauler, Sermons* (New York: Paulist Press, 1985).

74 Wolfhart Pannenberg, *Systematic Theology, Volume 1*, tr. Geoffrey W. Bromily (Grand Rapids: William B. Eerdmans Publishing Company, 1991), 314.

75 "Solid Declaration, Article viii: The Person of Christ" in *The Book of Concord, The Confessions of the Lutheran Church*, edited by Robert Kolb and Timothy J. Wengert (Minneapolis: Fortress Press, 2000), 619.

76 *The Suffering of the Impassible God*, 174-175.

77 "The Immutability of the God of Love and the Problem of Language Concerning the "Suffering of God" by Gilles Emery, O.P. in *Divine Impassibility and the Mystery of Human Suffering* (Grand Rapids: Wm. B. Eerdmans Publishing Co. 2009), 74-75.

MEDITATION IX

78 Nicolas Cabasilas, *The Life in Christ*, Translated from the Greek by Carmino J. deCatanzaro. With an Introduction by Boris Bobrinskoy (New York: St. Vladimir's Seminary Press, 1974), 190-191.

79 *Theologia Germanica of Martin Luther*, translated by Bengt Hoffman. Paulist Press, 1980. The page references in the body of the text throughout this Meditation are taken from this book. In 2003

a new English translation by David Blamires, *The Book of the Perfect Life* appeared. It is a more literal translation. He translates the first paragraph thus: "*Whoever wants to accept God, must and has to accept everything. Whoever wishes to be obedient, submissive and subject to God, must and has to be submissive, obedient and subject to all created things in a passive, not an active way. This must be done by silently resting in the very depth of one's soul and through a secret, hidden acceptance, bearing and accepting everything...*", 52. [emphasis added] I follow Hoffman, whose daring effort to render a translation that achieves dynamic equivalence honors the mystical vitality of the text.

80 St. Augustine, *The City of God*, Tr. By Marcus Dods, D.D. (New York: Random House, The Modern Library, 1950), 310.

81 Evelyn Underhill, *Mysticism, The Preeminent Study in the Nature and Development of Spiritual Consciousness*, Foreword by Ira Progoff (New York: Image Books, Doubleday, 1990), 178.

82 Underhill, *Mysticism*, p. 260.

83 Underhill, *Mysticism*, p. 196.

MEDITATION X

84 Paul Tillich, *Systematic Theology, Three Volumes in One* (Chicago Press, 1967) Volume One, 242.

85 John Paul II, *Roman Triptych, Meditations*, Translation by Jerzy Peteriewicz (Washington D.C.: United States Conference of Catholic Bishops, Inc. Libreria Editrice Vaticana, 2003), Meditation II, 20.

86 *Hadewijch, The Complete Works*, The Classics of Western Spirituality, Translated and Introduction by Mother Columba Hart, O.S.B., Preface by Paul Mommaers (New York: Paulist Press, 1980).

87 *Hadewijch, The Complete Works*, The Preface, xiv.

88 *Hadewijch, The Complete Works*, p. 82. I have numbered the three sets of couplets to facilitate the discussion.

89 *Hadewijch, The Complete Works*, The Introduction, 11f.

90 *Hadewijch, The Complete Works*, p. 83.

91 In Meditation X the page references in the text are from Ruus-broec, *The Spiritual Espousals and Other Works*.

92 *Hadewijch, The Complete Works*, p. 92.

93 "But he who is united to the Lord becomes one spirit with him." I Cor 6:17.

94 Thomas Merton, *No Man Is an Island* (New York: Fall River Press, 2003), 74.

95 Merton, *No Man Is an Island*, 74-75.

96 The five direct quotations that follow are from *The Little Book of Clarification*, which is printed in full in John Ruusbroec, *The Spiritual Espousals and Other Works*, 251-269. The page references in the text are from this book.

97 Louis Bouyer, *The Christian Mystery*, Translated by Illtyd Tre-thowan (Edinburgh: T&T Clark, 1990), 242.

CONCLUSION

98 I Cor 15:45

99 I Cor 6:17b.

BIBLIOGRAPHY OF PRIMARY SOURCES CITED

Meister Eckhart, *The Complete Mystical Works of Meister Eckhart*, Translated and Edited by Maurice O'C. Walshe. Revised with a Foreword by Bernard McGinn (New York: A Herder and Herder Book, The Crossroad Publishing Company, 2009).

Meister Eckhart, *Meister Eckhart: The Essential Sermons*, The Classics of Western Spirituality, Edited by Bernard McGinn (New York: Paulist Press, 1981).

John Tauler, *Johannes Tauler, Sermons*, The Classics of Western Spirituality, Translated by Mary Shady, Introduction by Josef Schmidt. Preface by Alois Haas (New York: Paulist Press, 1985).

John Tauler, *Spiritual Conferences*, Translated and Edited by Eric Colledge and Sister M. Jane, O.P. (Rockford: Tan Books and Publishers, Inc., 1978).

Steven Ozment, *Homo Spiritualis* (Leiden: E. J. Brill, 1969). Pages 13-46 contain valuable translations by Ozment of important excerpts of John Tauler's work.

The anonymous Frankfurt Priest, *The Theologia Germanica of Martin Luther*, The Classics of Western Spirituality, Translation, Introduction and Commentary by Bengt Hoffman. Preface by Bengt Hagglund (New York: Paulist Press, 1980).

The anonymous Frankfurt Priest, *The Book of the Perfect Life*, Translated and With an Introduction and Notes by David Blamires (Walnut Creek: AltaMira Press, 2003).

Henry Suso, *Bl. Henry Suso: Wisdoms Watch Upon the Hours*, The Fathers of the Church, Mediaeval Continuation, Translated by Edmond Colledge, O.S.A. (Washington D.C.: The Catholic University of America Press, 1994).

Henry Suso, *Henry Suso, The Exemplar, with Two German Sermons*, The Classics of Western Spirituality, Translated, Edited, and Introduced by Frank Tobin. Preface by Bernard McGinn (New York: Paulist Press, 1989).

John Ruusbroec, *John Ruusbroec: The Spiritual Espousals and Other Works*, The Classics of Western Spirituality, Introduction and Translation by James A. Wiseman, O.S.B. Preface by Louis Dupre (New York: Paulist Press, 1985).

ADDITIONAL SUGGESTED READING

The Christian mystical tradition is a long and varied one. Two anthologies that contain excerpts from the writings of the most well-known Christian mystics are *Light from Light, An Anthology of Christian Mysticism*, Second Edition, Completely Revised and Updated. Edited by Louis Dupre and James A. Wiseman, O.S.B. (New York: Paulist Press, 2001), and *Soundings in the Christian Mystical Tradition*, Edited by Harvey D. Egan, S.J. (Collegeville: Liturgical Press, 2010). These two books help to situate the Rhineland Mystics within the broader Christian mystical tradition. They also contain bibliographies that provide suggestions for further reading of these mystics in the English language.

www.ingramcontent.com/pod-product-compliance
Lightning Source LLC
LaVergne TN
LVHW051736080426
835511LV00018B/3096